Success in Literacy Reading Tests

UNDERSTANDING
YEAR 3
COMPREHENSION
Excellent for all Students, Teachers, Coaches and Parents

Authors

Alan Horsfield   M.Ed, B.A., B. Ed., Dip. Sch. Admin., TESOL, Teaching Cert.
Alan Horsfield has more than 35 years teaching experience in state and private schools in New South Wales and International Schools in Papua New Guinea. He was employed by UNSW (EAA) as an English Research Officer involved in the construction of school tests for English and Mathematics. Alan is a published writer of children's fiction, educational material and school texts.

Elaine Horsfield   M.A. (Theatre Studies), B.A. (Theatre Media), Teaching Cert.
Elaine Horsfield has more than 25 years teaching experience in Primary Schools both with the New South Wales Department of Education and in International Schools in Papua New Guinea. She worked with secondary students as coordinator of the NSW Talent Development Project. Elaine is a published writer of children's poetry and educational books.

Editor:
Warwick Marlin B.Sc. Dip.Ed.

Publisher:
Five Senses Education
ABN: 16 001 414437
2/195 Prospect Highway
Seven Hills NSW Australia 2147
sevenhills@fivesenseseducation.com.au
www.fivesenseseducation.com.au

Trade Enquiries:
Phone (02) 9838 9265
Fax (02) 9838 8982
Email: fsonline@fivesenseseducation.com.au

Understanding Year 3 Comprehension
ISBN: 978-1-76032-119-2
1ˢᵗ Edition: August 2015
Copyright: Alan Horsfield © Five Senses Education Pty. Ltd. © Warwick Marlin

AUTHOR'S ACKNOWLEDGEMENTS

Warwick Marlin, my editor, whose advice and guidance have been very much appreciated.

Roger Furniss, at Five Senses Education for publishing my books.

And above all, to **Jones**, my typesetter, for a high standard of typesetting, layout and artwork. A very special thank you for your time, patience, attention to detail, and overall quality of your work.

PARENTS

This book tells you what the teacher often does not have the time to explain in detail - the intricacies of a wide variation in text types and the testing strategies used by Australian testing institutions to assess progress in Literacy. It will give you confidence to support your children by reinforcing what is being taught in schools and what is being tested, especially Reading Comprehension.

TEACHERS

This book introduces text types and test question types Australian students should understand to maximise internal and external Reading Tests. Reading tests may involve comprehension as well as related grammar questions. It eliminates the need to wade through lengthy curriculum documents and it provides a clear easy to follow format for teachers to use. Teachers can confidently recommend this book to parents as it supports classroom activities and exercises.

B. Ed., Dip. Ed. PRIMARY SCHOOL TEACHERS

This book contains a variety of recognised primary school text types with question sets that will improve reading comprehension and improved results in reading tests. It acts as a quick reference book for teachers in the early years of teaching, when there is so much to learn.

"Tell me and I forget. Teach me and I remember. Involve me and I learn."
Benjamin Franklin

Understanding Year 3 Comprehension
A. Horsfield © Five Senses Education © W. Marlin

AVAILABILITY OF MATHEMATICS BOOKS

All of the Mathematics books below have been produced by the same editor and publisher, and in many cases the same author (Warwick Marlin). Therefore they all incorporate the same high presentation and philosophy. They can be purchased directly from Five Senses Education, but they are also available in most educational bookshops throughout NSW and Australia (and also some selected bookshops in New Zealand).

New National Curriculum titles

The eight school titles listed directly below have been rewritten and updated in recent years to closely follow the New National Curriculum. **'All levels'** means that the books have been written for students of most ability groups (weak, average and gifted). The graded tests at the end of each chapter ensure that students of most ability groups are extended to their full potential.

❑   YEAR 1   ALL LEVELS
❑   YEAR 2   ALL LEVELS
❑   YEAR 3   ALL LEVELS
❑   YEAR 4   ALL LEVELS
❑   YEAR 5   ALL LEVELS
❑   YEAR 6   ALL LEVELS
❑   YEAR 7   ALL LEVELS
❑   YEAR 8   ALL LEVELS

Other titles in this series

The titles listed below are also available, but they will be fully updated during 2014 and 2015 to also closely follow the new curriculum. However, in the meantime, please note, that these books still adequately address the main features of the new syllabus. We firmly believe that the major topics explained in these titles, and our user friendly presentation and development of the different topics, will always continue to form the vital foundations for all future study and applications of mathematics. This is especially so for the titles up to, and including, Year 10 Advanced.

❑   YEAR 9 & 10   INTERMEDIATE
❑   YEAR 9 & 10   ADVANCED
❑   YEAR 11 & 12   GENERAL MATHS
❑   YEAR 11   EXTENSION 1
❑   YEAR 12   EXTENSION 1

Also by the same Author and Editor (Warwick Marlin)

❑   ESSENTIAL EXERCISES YEAR 1   ALL LEVELS
❑   ESSENTIAL EXERCISES YEAR 2   ALL LEVELS
❑   ESSENTIAL EXERCISES YEAR 3   ALL LEVELS
❑   ESSENTIAL EXERCISES YEAR 4   ALL LEVELS
❑   ESSENTIAL EXERCISES YEAR 5   ALL LEVELS
❑   ESSENTIAL EXERCISES YEAR 6   ALL LEVELS

Developed & written in 2012, this excellent new series of books closely follows the Australian National Curriculum.

CONTENTS

Year 3 Comprehension Passages and Exercises

"So it is with children who learn to read fluently and well. They begin to take flight into whole new worlds as effortlessly as young birds take to the sky."

William James

Understanding Year 3 Comprehension
A. Horsfield © Five Senses Education © W. Marlin

UNDERSTANDING YEAR 3 ENGLISH TESTING

This is an important year in the child's education. Groundwork commenced in Year 2 leads to a more formal development of literacy understanding in Year 3. The school and the home continue to work closely together. It is important that the home has a positive attitude to school and education, and also provides support with an abundance of practical activities in an environment that stimulates curiosity and enjoyment in reading and writing. The more literacy experiences the child has, the more realistic and practical will be the child's foundation in Literacy in later years, and the more confidence the child will have.

It is in these early years the child continues to become a fluent reader and move from literal comprehension of text to the more abstract. What is implied becomes more and more important. This transition will vary from child to child. At times, we all read different 'messages' into text. It is also important to understand that we don't always grasp the intended meaning on a first reading. Re-reading is an important strategy.

Remember: Do not have unreal expectations of what your child can read. Don't 'push' too hard, especially with the more formal written work. Keep literacy fun, especially in reading then attitudes will be positive. At times it is fun to read something that is not so challenging!

The best way to succeed in any test is to practice.
An old Chinese proverb sums it up well:
> I hear, I forget;
> I see, I remember;
> I do, I understand.

I enjoy a little bit of recreational reading every day!

The NAPLAN testing program for Australian Schools treats three aspects of English.
Reading tests, which include the comprehension of a variety of text types,
Writing tests, which focus on writing a narrative, a persuasive text or a recount,
Language Conventions tests, which include Spelling, Punctuation and Grammar.

The English Curriculum is built around the three interrelated strands of Language, Literature and Literacy. They are interrelated in the 'real world'. As the Australian Curriculum states, "Teaching and learning programs should balance and integrate all three strands"(see: http://www.australiancurriculum.edu.au/Year 3).

This book is based on Year levels not Stages. (There are three basic primary school stages. Year 3 and Year 4 make up Stage 2.) In Year 3 there is a developing emphasis on comprehending a variety of text types. Not all text types get the same attention. The study of persuasive text is more complex and subtle than, say, following directions. As families and society are a complex mix of differing experiences, children will have different exposure to different text types. Individual children will develop different strengths and weaknesses.

This book focuses specifically on Reading but the skills learned in Reading can assist in the development of the child's Writing skills. The skills learned in the Language Convention strand can improve both Reading and Writing.

That is why we have included a Literacy Tip **(Lit Tip)** component following each set of questions. These may help with any Language Convention questions that come up in standardised reading tests as well adding 'tricks' that may improve the quality of Writing test responses.

HOW TO USE THIS BOOK EFFECTIVELY

As stated, this book's primary aim is to improve Reading comprehension with some input into Writing and Language Conventions. Obviously the Speaking, Listening and Handwriting strands are not included.

The passages are not selected in any specific order but are intended to present a wide variation of text types. Those most likely to be part of the testing situation are treated more often. The text type is shown at the top of each passage as well as in the **List of comprehension passages and exercises** chart that follows. The more difficult passages tend to be towards the end of the book.

There will be differences of focus from school to school, as teachers tend to select topics in varying sequences according to their program at a particular time in the year. Some students may be involved in accelerated promotion, enrichment or remedial activities.

ABOUT THE EXERCISES

The intent of the 40 passages is to provide one passage per week for each school week. This should not impinge too much on obligations set by the school/class teacher for homework and research. There is one easier **practice passage** provided to make the child aware of a range of question types that may be encountered.

Children need not work through the exercisers from 1 to 40 in the order in which they are presented in this book. There is the option of practicing a particular text type, e.g. poetry.

The Comprehension Answers and the Lit Tip Answers are on separate pages at the back of the book.

Texts can be either **Factual** or **Literary** texts.
Factual texts inform, report, instruct or persuade by giving facts and information.
Literary texts entertain or cause an emotional response by using language to create mental images.

Year 3 questions types often include the skills of:
- **Locating** such things as information, a sequence of events, literary techniques, grammar conventions and vocabulary features,

- **Identifying** genres, the purpose of a text, literary techniques, appropriate punctuation, word meanings,

- **Interpreting** visual information, multiple pieces of information, language style,

- **Inferring** next events in a text, reasons for a character's action, outcomes, the effect of tense and person, and

- **Synthesising** the tone of a text, the main idea in a text, a character's motivation, the writer's opinion, the intended audience for a text.

These above skills are more or less arranged in an order of difficulty.

Alan Horsfield M.Ed., B.A., B. Ed., Dip. Sch. Admin., TESOL, Teaching Cert.
Elaine Horsfield M. A. (Theatre Studies), B. A. (Theatre Media), Teaching Cert

Understanding Year 3 Comprehension
A. Horsfield © Five Senses Education © W. Marlin

TEST SOURCES

The questions, information and practice provided by this book will benefit the student sitting for the following tests. Year 3 is a NAPLAN testing year.

Externally produced tests

NAPLAN (National Assessment - Literacy and Numeracy) Used Australia wide.
PAT (-R) (Progressive Achievements Tests - Reading)
ICAS (International Competitions and Assessments for Schools) Run by EAA.
Selective Schools and High Schools Placement Tests (Most states have tests specific to that state's educational policy.)
Scholarship Tests
ACER (Australian Council for Educational Research) Scholarship tests (Most states have tests specific to that state's educational policy)
AusVELS (Australian Curriculum in Victoria Essential Learning Standards)
Independent Assessment Agencies (e.g. Academic Assessment Services)
ISA (International Schools Assessment) run by ACER
There may be a number of other independent, external sources for literacy testing.

School produced tests

year tests   class tests   school tests

Information provided in this book may also be beneficial in certain competitions run by commercial enterprises. A number of commercial publishers also provide books of practice tests.

The purpose of testing

Testing has a variety of purposes and the purpose will often determine the type of test administered. Tests may be used to
* determine what the student has learned
* rank students in order of ability
* select the most worthy student for a school or class
* determine the strength and weakness of classroom teaching
* determine any 'short-comings' in a school's educational program
* ascertain the effectiveness of certain teaching strategies
* evaluate the effectiveness of departmental/official syllabuses

English Achievement Standard

By the end of Year 3, students understand how content can be organised using different text structures depending on the purpose of the text. They understand how language features, images and vocabulary choices are used for different effects. They read texts that contain varied sentence structures, a range of punctuation conventions, and images that provide additional information. They identify literal and implied meaning connecting ideas in different parts of a text. They select information, ideas and events in texts that relate to their own lives and to other texts.

Specifically Year 3 students will:
Discuss texts in which characters, events and settings are portrayed in different ways, and speculate on the authors' reason (ACELT1594)
Draw connections between personal experiences and the worlds of texts, and share responses with others (ACELT1596)
Develop criteria for establishing personal preferences for literature (ACELT1598)
Discuss how language is used to describe the settings in texts, and explore how the settings shape the events and influence the mood of the narrative (ACELT1599)
Discuss the nature and effects of some language devices used to enhance meaning and shape the reader's reaction, including rhythm and onomatopoeia in poetry and prose (ACELT1600)

(**Adapted from** http://www.australiancurriculum.edu.au/english/curriculum/f-10?layout=1)

A BRIEF SUMMARY OF SOME QUESTION FORMATS AND STYLES.

Look at the text from the narrative, **The Duckling**, as a text for a set of questions.

"Stop swimming so that I can count you," quacked Mother Duck as her new batch of ducklings paddled about <u>cheerfully</u> by the reeds in the pond. She counted just five ducklings! "I knew it! Daisy is missing. We have to find her straight away."

Daisy often disappeared. She liked to swim at the end of the line and often got left behind or just paddle off exploring on her own. Later Grandpa Drake waddled to the_____(4)_____ to investigate. Where was Daisy?

Many tests are based on multiple-choice responses. You are given a choice of four (sometimes three) possible answers (options) to choose from.
Some will take the form of a question: You may have to **circle a letter** or **shade a bubble**.

1. Why did Mother duck stop swimming??
   A   to count her ducklings
   B   to have a rest
   C   to watch Grandpa Drake
   D   to wait for her ducklings

The question could have been framed so that you have to complete a sentence.
2. Mother duck stopped swimming to
   A   count her ducklings   B   have a rest

   C   watch Grandpa Drake   D   wait for her ducklings

Some questions may have to do with word or phrase meanings.
3. Choose the word that could best replace *cheerfully* as used in the text.
   A   lazily   B   willingly   C   carefully   D   happily
(Did you notice the different lay-out of the options? They were across the page.)

4. Which word would best go in the space (4) in the last line?
   A   shed   B   bank   C   farm   D   boat

Sometimes you might have to work out the order in which events occurred.
5. Write the numbers 1 to 4 in the boxes to show the correct order in which events occurred in the text. The first one (1) has been done for you.

1	Mother Duck took her ducklings for a paddle on the pond.
	Grandpa Drake came to investigate.
	Mother Duck stopped to count her ducklings.
	Mother Duck wondered if Daisy Duck was missing.

Some questions are called free response questions. You will have to write an answer.
6. How many ducklings did Mother Duck have? Write your answer on the line? _____

Sometimes you might have to decide if something is TRUE or FALSE.
7. Tick the box to show if this statement is TRUE or FALSE

Grandpa Duck knew where Daisy was. TRUE ☐   FALSE ☐

There will be times when you will have to read the whole text and make a judgement.
8. What word best describes how Mother Duck felt when she counted her ducklings?
   A   scared   B   glad   C   worried   D   angry

9. Sometimes you may have to decide if a text is FACT or FICTION.

Answers: 1. A   2. A   3. D   4. B   5. (1, 4, 3, 2)   6. 6   7. FALSE   8. C

Understanding Year 3 Comprehension
A. Horsfield © Five Senses Education © W. Marlin

This is a practice page. (The answers follow the questions)

Read the narrative *Parrot Muesli.*

Parrot Muesli

"Know what Martin?" Mum asked cheerily next morning as she dished out her latest kitchen <u>concoction</u>. "Home made muesli."

She watches too many cooking shows on TV!

The mixture in my breakfast bowl looked like birdseed with a sawdust sprinkle.

Even the milk in the bowl seemed unable to soak into the stuff and soften it up.

Was I really hungry enough to eat breakfast? I was, but not the stuff in my bowl. I've seen better on the floor of our cocky's cage!

I sat glumly watching the mixture as I swirled it around slowly with my spoon. I'd have to eat some soon. I decided to separate all the ingredients. I pushed some dirty brown chunks to the twelve o'clock position in my bowl - as far from me as possible.

Bits of faded coloured dried fruit I brought down to the six o'clock position. The sultanas went to the three o'clock and a little pile of sawdust went west.

At least with alphabet soup I could find words. That can be a problem too because Dad reckons I make words I shouldn't be using.

I suddenly realised Mum was silent and I could feel her eyes boring into my thoughts. I forced the first spoonful into my___(7)___.

Understanding Narratives

(**Note:** The answers follow the questions for this Practice passage.)

1. Who was expected to eat the Muesli?
    A   Martin's father
    B   the pet cocky
    C   Martin's mother
    D   Martin

2. Why is Martin swirling around the ingredients in his breakfast bowl?
    A   he is separating the good bits from the bad bits
    B   he is trying to find all the sawdust
    C   he is afraid to taste the muesli
    D   he is waiting for his mother to start eating

3. Which word best explains how Martin's mother feels about her new muesli?
    A   she is worried
    B   she is excited
    C   she is relaxed
    D   she is nervous

4. In the first paragraph you read that Mum dished out her latest kitchen <u>concoction</u>.
What is a concoction?
    A   a mixture of ingredients
    B   food for a cocky
    C   a TV cooking show
    D   anything that tastes awful

5. Martin pushed the ingredient that looked like sawdust to the
    A   6 o'clock position in his bowl
    B   centre of his breakfast bowl
    C   western side of his bowl
    D   opposite side of his bowl

6. After separating the muesli ingredients in his bowl Martin
    A   felt he had to eat some muesli
    B   fed the pet cocky
    C   made words in his alphabet soup
    D   pushed his bowl towards his mother

7. A word has been deleted from the last sentence of the text.
Which word would be best suited to the space (7)?
    A   bowl   B   mouth   C   shoe   D   bag

Answers: 1. D   2. C   3. B   4. A   5. C   6. A   7. B

Understanding Year 3 Comprehension
A. Horsfield © Five Senses Education © W. Marlin

Year 3 Comprehension Passages and Exercises

Each of the 40 passages has a set of eight questions – comprehension and language questions, based upon that text. Following the questions is a section called **Lit Tip** (short for Literacy Tips). These are gems of information that are intended to develop the student's responses to Language Conventions questions arising in texts and tests. They may also be beneficial when answering questions in Language Convention (Grammar) papers or when completing Writing assessment tasks.

Understanding Year 3 Comprehension
A. Horsfield © Five Senses Education © W. Marlin

Simone had to write a recount as part of a class project. This is what she wrote.

Daintree River Ferry

We were camping in the small sugar town of Mossman when Dad suggested we do some sightseeing. Dad is a bit of an explorer. He suggested we take a short trip to Alexandra Range Lookout in the Daintree National Park.

Sugarcane is taken to the Mossman sugar mill by sugar trains. The narrow railway line goes right through the town. We had to wait for a long sugar train to chug across the main street before we could continue on our journey north. Dad took a photo.

We crossed the Mossman River bridge and headed north. We passed by fields of tall, green sugarcane before coming to the turn-off to the lookout.

We arrived at the Daintree River. There was no bridge but there was a car ferry. A sign warned people not to paddle or swim in the river while waiting for the ferry. Crocodiles! While we were waiting for the ferry to cross Dad took more photos. Dad drove onto the ferry and the gates were shut. You have to stay in your car as you cross. It was quite exciting but we didn't see any crocs!

After driving off we were soon climbing up a mountain covered in tropical jungle. The trees hung over the narrow winding road.

We found the small lookout. From there we could see where the Daintree River wound its way through kilometres of mangrove swamps to the sea. No wonder the river is full of crocodiles.

Because it was hot Mum and I quenched our thirst before we began our return trip - while we waited for Dad to take lots more photos!

Photo: Alan Horsfield

Understanding Recounts

Circle a letter or write an answer for questions 1 to 7.

1. Simone's family was in the town of Mossman
   - A   for a camping holiday
   - B   to have a ride on a train
   - C   to take photos
   - D   for a visit to the sugar mill

2. What is the name of the first river the family crossed before reaching the lookout?

   Writer your answer in the box. [＿＿＿＿＿＿＿＿＿] River

3. Where did the family see a sugarcane train?
   - A   near the Daintree Ferry
   - B   in the main street of Mossman
   - C   by the camping ground at Mossman
   - D   at Alexandra Range Lookout

4. What did Simone's father enjoy doing?
   - A   looking for crocodiles
   - B   riding on a ferry
   - C   watching sugar cane trains
   - D   taking photographs

5. Simone saw the the crocodile warning sign
   - A   in the camping grounds
   - B   near the Mossman River bridge
   - C   at the ferry crossing
   - D   by the mangroves swamps

6. You read that after the family crossed the bridge they *headed north*.
   What would be a suitable word to replace *headed* as used in the text?
   - A   faced
   - B   aimed
   - C   proceeded
   - D   looked

7. What was the last thing Simone did before the family returned to Mossman?
   - A   climbed up a mountain
   - B   quenched her thirst
   - C   took photos of mangroves
   - D   looked for crocodiles

Lit Tip 1 – Improve your Literacy skills   **Capital letters**

Capital letters are the most common form of punctuation.
Capital letters are used for:
- the first word of a sentence and after a full stop: This is mine!
- proper nouns (the actual names of people places and things): Canberra
- brand names: Vegemite
- official titles and official religions: Captain Jones, Buddha
- Adjectives made from proper nouns (e.g. Victoria - Victorian floods)

Underline the words that should have a capital letter.
we saw sir peter green in perth on sunday. he was eating a big mac!

Understanding Year 3 Comprehension
A. Horsfield © Five Senses Education © W. Marlin

What is a Bunyip?

Long before Europeans walked this country, bunyips were believed to lurk in swamps, creeks, riverbeds, waterholes and billabongs. They are mythological creatures from

Aboriginal folklore. The word bunyip literally means devil or spirit. The origin of the word bunyip has been traced to the language of Aboriginal people of South-Eastern Australia.

The bunyip was mostly described as a creature that 'had shining, evil eyes and a bellowing voice'. Other descriptions were of large animals, with bodies resembling crocodiles with emu-like heads that walked on their hind legs. Some said they had flippers, a horse-like head and a tail and tusks like a walrus.

Aborigines thought they could hear bunyip cries at night. It was a belief that bunyips took humans, preferably women, as a food source when their supplies were low. They blamed the Bunyip for spreading diseases in river areas.

Bunyips are a figment of Aboriginal imagination. It is most likely the cries they heard in the night belonged to possums or koalas. The cries of women supposedly being captured may have been calls of a barking owl.

Fact or fantasy? One thing is certain, the stories will continue to be told around camp-fires on the banks of the western rivers or by lonely billabongs in the bush.

Sources: http://www.lenntech.com/water-mythology.htm, http://en.wikipedia.org/wiki/Bunyip

http://www.murrayriver.com.au/about-the-murray/bunyips/

Understanding Explanations

Circle a letter to answer questions 1 to 7.

1. Which word would best describe a bunyip?

   A   fearsome   B   shy   C   friendly   D   timid

2. It is most likely the cries in the night Aboriginal people heard were really the

   A   noises made by campers at waterholes
   B   calls of native animals
   C   cries of people captured by bunyips
   D   sounds made by water spirits

3. Bunyips are said to live

   A   in riverside camps   B   in waterholes
   C   with Aboriginal people   D   among native animals

4. There is no actual description of a bunyip because bunyips

   A   only leave their hiding places at night
   B   spend most of their life under water
   C   are easily frightened by strange bush noises
   D   are a figment of Aboriginal imagination

5. The descriptions of the bunyip do **NOT** include images of

   A   creatures that look like giant emus
   B   beasts with crocodile-like bodies
   C   ape-like creatures
   D   hippopotamuses with horse-like heads

6. Which word from the text has an opposite meaning to the word *fact*?

   A   fantasy
   B   belief
   C   figment
   D   certain

7. The word *lurk* as used in the first paragraph refers to the

   A   retelling of aboriginal stories
   B   callings for help from captured people
   C   searching around waterholes for food
   D   waiting in hiding to ambush a victim

Lit Tip 2 – Improve your Literacy skills   **Alphabetical order 1**

This is the alphabet; A B C D E F G H I J K L M N O P Q R S T U V W X Y Z

Words in a dictionary are in alphabetical order.

Fill in the missing letters: **1.** G _____ I J K L M _____ O   **2.** Q R _____ T U V W _____ Y

The first letter of a word determines its place in the dictionary: ape comes before zebra.

Start by looking at the first letter.

3. Here is a list of words in alphabetical order: bat, frog, lizard, _____, walrus

Circle the word that would best fill the space: cat, ant, seal, yak, goanna

Understanding Year 3 Comprehension
A. Horsfield © Five Senses Education © W. Marlin

3   Read the poem *Shopping With Dad* by Elaine Horsfield.

Shopping With Dad

Sometimes on a Saturday Mum has to work
So we do the shopping with Dad
We hop in the car and drive down to the mall
And check out what's there to be had.

We don't have a list 'cause it's more fun to see
What the shops have displayed on the shelf.
And Dad says that lists just restrict your ideas
So it's better to think for yourself.

We each take a trolley and choose our own row
Then slowly we walk down the aisle.
We fill up our trolley with heaps of good things.
Choosing can take quite a while.

When we get to the end we find Dad waiting there.
His trolley is filled to the top.
He checks what we've got and sends some of it back.
Dad says we must know when to stop.

We go through the checkout and Dad pays the bill
Then we load up the boot of the car.
And if we've been sensible with what we chose,
Dad will buy us a chocolate bar.

At home we pack everything up on the shelves
And call Mum to check that it's right.
She looks in the cupboard and says with a smile
"I think we might eat out tonight."

Elaine Horsfield

Understanding Poetry

Circle a letter or write an answer for questions 1 to 7.

1. Dad does the shopping when
   - A   Mum is at work
   - B   the children are at school
   - C   the supermarket shelves are empty
   - D   Mum comes home from work

2. Which option best describes how Dad reacts to shopping?
   - A   he finds it boring
   - B   he makes it fun
   - C   he thinks it's a waste of time
   - D   he gets confused

3. When does dad know he has finished shopping?
   - A   when he has got everything on his list
   - B   when he has run out of money
   - C   when his trolley is full to the top
   - D   when there is no more room in the car boot

4. Which statement is CORRECT?
   - A   The children don't like shopping with Dad.
   - B   Dad buys everything the children put in their trolley.
   - C   Dad thinks a list is important when he goes shopping.
   - D   The children are allowed to do some choosing of items

5. Which line from the poem shows that children are **NOT** careful shoppers?
   - A   We hop in the car and drive down to the mall
   - B   We fill up our trolley with heaps of good things.
   - C   At home we pack everything up on the shelves
   - D   When we get to the end we find Dad waiting there.

6. Which word from the poem rhymes with *aisle*?

   Write your answer in the box. [   ]

7. What does Dad do before they put the things they have bought in the car?
   - A   he gives the children a chocolate bar
   - B   he puts some of his purchases back on the shelf
   - C   he pays for the goods in the trolleys
   - D   he takes the family out for a meal

Lit Tip 3 – Improve your Literacy skills   **Rhyme**

Most poetry makes use of rhyme (but not all poems).
Most rhyme depends on the end sound of a word. Often the words end with the same letters,
e.g. f<u>at</u> and c<u>at</u>, h<u>atch</u> and c<u>atch</u>
Same word endings do **not** mean the words always rhyme, e.g. w<u>as</u> and h<u>as</u>

Circle the word that does **not** rhyme in these lists.
1. cow, now ,low, wow, pow   2. laid, said, raid, maid, paid
3. four, more, sure, war, pure   4. sum, come, home, dumb, scrum

Understanding Year 3 Comprehension
A. Horsfield © Five Senses Education © W. Marlin

4 Read the Aesop fable, ***The Mice's Meeting.***

> Aesop was an Ancient Greek storyteller. He lived about 2500 years ago. It is believed he told over 600 different stories, many of them as fables. This is one of them.

The Mice's Meeting

Once upon a time a number of mice were troubled by a rather nasty cat. They called a meeting to find the best way to protect themselves from the cat menace. The cat had been responsible for catching and eating a number of their friends and relations.

At the meeting various plans were discussed but eventually rejected until, at last, a small mouse proposed that a bell should be hung around the cruel cat's neck. This way the mice would have plenty of warning of the cat's movement and they could escape to their holes.

The idea was joyfully received by all the mice except for one old mouse who had listened carefully to all the discussions.

When all the excitement subsided and the meeting became quiet he slowly raised himself up. All the mice turned to look at him.

"I consider the plan to be a very clever one. I feel sure it would be quite successful if carried out. What I would like to know is which brave mouse is going to put the bell on the cat?" he asked softly.

Silently the mice looked at one another but no one volunteered to put the bell on the cat.

Understanding Narratives

Circle a letter or write an answer for questions 1 to 7.

1. The mice were having a meeting to
   - A   find a method to get rid of the cat
   - B   devise a scheme to put a bell on the cat
   - C   find a way to protect themselves from the cat
   - D   investigate safer places to live

2. What was the purpose of putting a bell on the cat?
   - A   it was a gift to show the cat the mice wanted to be friends
   - B   the bell would give a warning ring whenever the cat moved
   - C   the cat would be pleased to wear a bell decoration
   - D   bells create sounds that the mice and cat would appreciate

3. When mice at the meeting heard the small mouse's suggestion they were
   - A   excited
   - B   suspicious
   - C   thoughtful
   - D   dismayed

4. Fables often have a lesson than can be learned.
   What would be the lesson in this fable?
   - A   One cat is smarter than any group of mice.
   - B   Little people have the best ideas.
   - C   Meetings are the best way to solve problems.
   - D   It is easier to make a suggestion than carry it out.

5. The cat was at the meeting held by the mice.
   Is this statement TRUE or FALSE? Tick a box.

   TRUE ☐   FALSE ☐

6. The mice were silent after the old mouse spoke because
   - A   no mouse was brave enough to carry out the plan
   - B   he was old and he should be listened to respectfully
   - C   the mice did not listen to what the old mouse said
   - D   the mice were being quiet so that the cat couldn't hear them

7. What part of speech is the word *plan* as used in paragraph 5?
   - A   verb   B   noun   C   adjective   D   adverb

Lit Tip 4 – Improve your Literacy skills   **Alphabetical order 2**

Before you start check **Lit Tip 2**.
The order of the words in a dictionary depends upon the first letter of the word.
What if the words begin with the same letter? You look at the second letter!
Look at the underlined letters in these words: art, aim, act, add, age, ape
Act has c as the second letter. The c comes before all the other second letters.
The correct alphabetical order for these words is: a**c**t, a**d**d, a**g**e, a**i**m, a**p**e, a**r**t

Write the numbers 1 to 5 under these words to show their alphabetical order.

1. cut, cry, can, cent, cop
☐ ☐ ☐1☐ ☐ ☐

2. tree, then, tack, tune, tiny
☐ ☐ ☐ ☐ ☐

Understanding Year 3 Comprehension
A. Horsfield © Five Senses Education © W. Marlin

5 Read the procedure *Wash Your Hands!*

Wash Your Hands!

It is important to wash your hands often.
You should always wash them:

- if they are dirty
- after sneezing or coughing
- before and after handling food
- after going to the toilet
- if you have been playing with pets
- after touching commonly handled items
- after <u>manual</u> labour or gardening

How to Wash Your Hands

- Wet your hands with warm running water then lather with soap.

- Rub soap over all areas of your hands, including between the fingers, thumbs and backs of hands.

- Wash for at least 10 seconds.

- Rinse hands well and dry thoroughly on a clean cloth or paper towel.

- If soap and water are not available, an antiseptic based hand rub may be used. Remember these products do not work well if you have dirt on your hands.

Antiseptic based hand rubs (often called alcohol based hand rubs) are an alternative to washing hands with soap and water. Many preparations are available, including gel, foam, and liquid solutions. They are often used when out camping or when___(7)___.
Some come in a pump-action container.

Adapted from: http://www.wikihow.com/Wash-Your-Hands

http://www.cdc.gov/handwashing/when-how-handwashing.html

Understanding Procedures

Circle a letter or write an answer for questions 1 to 7.

1. You read in the *How to Wash Your Hands* section to *lather with soap*.
    When you *lather with soap* you
    - A   cause a frothy white mass of bubbles to form
    - B   add a thin layer of soap to your hands
    - C   spread soap thickly on the palms of your hands
    - D   place the soap into warm water to make it softer

2. Draw a ring around a word to answer this question.
    Are soap and water always needed to have clean, germ free hands?   YES   NO

3. What is a *gel*? (last paragraph)
    - A   a liquid soap
    - B   a foaming cleanser
    - C   a jelly like substance
    - D   a type of make-up

4. In the last line in the section **Wash your hands!** the word *manual* is underlined.
    What is manual labour?
    - A   work done with the hands
    - B   work done by a man
    - C   work that requires strength
    - D   work requiring two labourers

5. Write the numbers 1 to 4 in the boxes to show the correct order in which you should wash your hands. The first one (1) has been done for you.

	rub soap over your wet hands
	wash your hands for at least 10 seconds
1	wet your hands with warm running water
	rinse your hands before drying them on a dry cloth

6. Which of these would **NOT** be a commonly handled item?
    - A   doorknob
    - B   shopping trolley
    - C   money
    - D   supermarket frozen food

7. A word has been deleted from the text.
    Which word would be best suited to the space (7)?
    - A   sleeping   B   travelling   C   swimming   D   cleaning

---

Understanding Year 3 Comprehension
A. Horsfield © Five Senses Education © W. Marlin

Olivia's Birthday Invitation Card

Olivia handed out her invites to her friends. This is one of them.

Front

You are invited to

Olivia's
7th Birthday

to make mini pizzas in
our very own pizza oven!

Bring your own red
and white apron.

WHEN?

Sunday 15 July

Back

Hi, <u>Judy</u>
Hope you can come.
You may bring along
any favourite
topping you would
like on your mini
pizza but we will
have plenty of
things to add!

RSVP
Monday 10 July

Mum looks after the kitchen and Dad will look after the oven.

Understanding Transactions

Circle a letter or write an answer for questions 1 to 7.

1. The mini pizzas for the party will be made by
   - A   Olivia's mother
   - B   Olivia's father
   - C   children who attend the party
   - D   Olivia

2. The pattern of red and white (▨) squares is most likely meant to look like the pattern on a
   - A   tablecloth
   - B   curtain
   - C   pizza oven
   - D   an ingredients container

3. Who was this invitation for?

   Write your answer in the box.

4. On which day do people who receive an invitation have to let Olivia know if they can come to her party?
   - A   3 July
   - B   7 July
   - C   10 July
   - D   15 July

5. What will Olivia's mother most likely be doing at the party?
   - A   cooking the pizzas
   - B   making the pizzas
   - C   adding ingredients to the pizzas
   - D   organising the children making pizzas

6. Which of these words from the invitation is a compound word?
   - A   Monday
   - B   birthday
   - C   favourite
   - D   topping

7. It is suggested that children coming to the party bring an apron. The apron is most likely meant
   - A   as a present for Olivia
   - B   as a gift to Olivia's mother and father
   - C   to protect the children if they go near the pizza oven
   - D   to keep the children's clothes clean

Lit Tip 6 – Improve your Literacy skills   **Question marks (?)**

Put a question mark (?) at the end of a sentence that is a direct question.

Example: *How are you today?*

Questions can be made up of many words or just one word, e.g. *What?*

Question sentences often start with words such as *what, how, when, where, why, which* as well as *can, did, will* and others.

Not all sentences that begin with these words have to be a question.

This is not a question: *When we got to Cairns I was asleep.*

Add the correct stop.

1. May I have a piece of cake ( )   2. Why it happened I'll never know ( )

Understanding Year 3 Comprehension
A. Horsfield © Five Senses Education © W. Marlin

The Cassowary

Cassowaries live in tropical lowland rainforests and dense highland forests of northern Australia. The bird is rarely seen in the wild.

The main threats to the survival of the cassowary are deforestation and the introduction of dogs, foxes, cats and pigs which eat cassowary eggs. The cassowary may soon become an endangered species.

Cassowaries are slightly smaller than emus and ostriches. They grow to 1.8m and have a mass of 55kg. Females are larger than males.

Its large body is covered in black feathers. It has bluish skin on the head and has a reddish neck. Upper legs are blue while lower parts are grey.

The cassowary has a helmet like crest (casque) on its head. It can be 15cm long and 16cm in height. The casque is used for self-defence. It prevents skull injuries during fights but also makes it easier to move through the dense vegetation.

Cassowaries cannot fly due to lack of chest bone that supports muscles used for flying. They can run at 50km/hour and jump to 1.5m into the air.

Breeding takes place from June to October. Males build the nests. The females lay between 3 and 8 greenish-blue eggs.

Females are not responsible for the survival of eggs or young birds. Males are in charge of hatching the eggs that lasts 50 days. Males then take care of the chicks for a year.

Adapted from: http://www.softschools.com/facts/animals/cassowary_facts/306/

Understanding Reports

Circle a letter or write an answer for questions 1 to 7.

1. According to the text what might cause the cassowary to become extinct?

   A destruction of tropical forest
   B weather in tropical forests
   C damage to their protective helmet
   D shortage of nest eggs

2. Which part of the cassowary is its casque?

   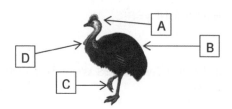

3. These are the three large flightless birds.

   emu   ostrich   cassowary

   Draw a ring around the one that is the smallest.

4. According to information in the text which statement is CORRECT?

   A The female cassowary cares for the chicks.
   B Cassowary parents share the nesting time to hatch the eggs.
   C The cassowary is a large flightless bird.
   D Cassowaries eat their own eggs.

5. What colour is the upper legs of a cassowary?

   A black   B blue   C grey   D red

6. Why are cassowaries rarely seen?

   A they have tropical forest colourings
   B they fly off when people come near
   C they spend a lot of time on nests
   D they live in thick, tropical forests

7. The term *in the wild* as used in paragraph 1 means

   A unable to be tamed   B a natural environment
   C having a bad temper   D being unpredictable

Lit Tip 7 – Improve your Literacy skills   **Explanation Marks (!)**

The exclamation mark (!) is a punctuation mark and is often used after an exclamation
(or interjection) to indicate strong feelings or loudly spoken words. It often marks the end of a sentence. **Example:** Hey! Get off the grass!
Can you 'hear' in your mind the difference between the next two sentences?
1. The guide said, "This way."   2. The guide said, "This way!"

Add exclamation marks to these sentences and then say them aloud.
Get out _   Don't do that _   I was wrong _   We want some more _
Writing tip. Don't put too many exclamations in your writing. It can be boring.

Understanding Year 3 Comprehension
A. Horsfield © Five Senses Education © W. Marlin

Leap Year Day

Leap Year Day is 29 February. Someone born on 29 February was born on leap day or leap year day.

A leap year is a year like 2016 or 2020. They come every four years.

It has 366 days, not 365.

Many people are born in a leap year. It lasts all year. Leap day babies were born on leap day. That is rare. In fact, the chances are 1 in 1500.

You don't have to be born on February 29 to enjoy leap day. It's an extra day for everyone!

> Thirty days have September,
>
> April, June, and November;
>
> February has 28 alone,
>
> All the rest have 31,
>
> Except leap year, that's the time,
>
> When February's days are 29.

What do Leap Day babies call themselves?

They are Leap Day babies, not leap year babies. There's a big difference! They were born on leap day - 29 February.

When do leap day babies celebrate their birthday?

In leap years, they celebrate on 29 February. That's every 4 years!

In off years, they can celebrate on 28 February because they were born in February. However, they were also born the day after the 28th so they can celebrate on 1 March if they want to. Or, both because they can! And some do!

Many countries have laws defining which date a person born on 29 February officially becomes an adult (18 years old in Australia). In New Zealand the official birthday falls on 28 February in common years. In the United Kingdom, they have to wait until 1 March.

http://en.wikipedia.org/wiki/February_29

http://www.timeanddate.com/date/leap-day-timeline.html

Understanding Explanations

Circle a letter or write an answer for questions 1 to 7.

1. Which of these months has thirty days?

   A   January   B   February

   C   March   D   April

2. What is the date of leap day?

   A   28 February   B   29 February

   C   1 March   D   30 March

3. Every baby born in a **leap year** is a **leap day** baby.

   Is this statement TRUE or FALSE? Tick a box.   TRUE ☐ FALSE ☐

4. In the subsection **When do Leap Day babies celebrate their birthday?** the text refers to *off* years.

   An *off* year is

   A   any year that is not a leap year

   B   a very unpleasant year

   C   a year that is a long way off

   D   those years when birthdays are celebrated

5. What is a *common year*? (see last paragraph)

   A   the year a person turns 18

   B   the year when February has 29 days

   C   a year with 365 days

   D   a year when most babies are born

6. The text suggests that people born on 29 February

   A   can celebrate their birthdays twice in some years

   B   miss out on celebrating their birth date

   C   are not sure when they turn 18 years of age

   D   do not get a year older each year

7. What word could be used instead of *rare* (paragraph 2) that has a similar meaning?

   A   odd   B   uncommon   C   special   D   unexpected

Lit Tip 8 – Improve your Literacy skills   **Common nouns**

Common nouns are words used for referring to people, places or things.
Examples: pirate, girl, bay, forest, star, truck
We can see, hear, feel, smell and even taste 'nouns'.
Examples: horse, whistle, ache, scent, flavour
Not all common nouns are the names of things that can be seen or touched.
Examples: air, space, ideas, lecture, stench, chill, music, tang

Draw a line under the common nouns in this sentence.
A shirt and cap were hanging in the sunlight on a line held by two pegs.

Understanding Year 3 Comprehension
A. Horsfield © Five Senses Education © W. Marlin

9　Read the play script **Dad's Lesson.**

Dad's Lesson

Characters:　*Mr Wheeler, four children aged between 6 years and 9 years (Peter Wheeler and younger sister Jenny, neighbours Tina and Mick).*

Scene:　*Mr Wheeler is with four children standing on the edge of a road.*

All five people are facing the audience as if that is the roadway.

Mr Wheeler:　It's important you know how to cross the road. There are common sense rules to follow, especially going to school.

Tina:　My Mum always drives me to school.

Mr Wheeler:　You never know, one day you might be allowed to walk to school. The first thing is to stand near the <u>verge</u> of the road so that drivers will see you.

Mick:　Why don't we use pedestrian crossings? Cars stop when you're on a crossing.

Peter:　(*pointing*) One up there! We'd be safe using that.

Mr Wheeler:　There's not always a crossing nearby. Jenny, put the phone away!

Tina:　There's one outside the school and traffic wardens tell us when to cross.

Mr Wheeler:　One day you will have to cross this street on your own. You should know what to do.

Jenny:　Why don't we cross at the lights at the intersection?

Peter:　Mum says lights are good because there are buttons to push.

Mr Wheeler:　Really! Let's just pretend the lights aren't working and you need to cross this street right here! (*The children give him a puzzled look.*)

Mr Wheeler:　This is important. Here's what you do. You look to the right. You look to the left then you look to the right again. If there are no cars coming you can cross safely.

Peter:　But Dad -

Mr Wheeler:　(*annoyed*) What now?

Peter:　We don't have to do that. (*Mr Wheeler frowns.*)

Peter:　(*grinning*) It's a one-way street!

Understanding Play Scripts

Circle a letter to answer questions 1 to 7.

1. The action for this short play is set
    A   outside a school
    B   in a one-way street
    C   at a pedestrian crossing
    D   in a car park

2. Which character was using a mobile phone?
    A   Jenny   B   Tina   C   Mick   D   Peter

3. What part of the road is the *verge*?
    A   the sealed section cars drive on
    B   the footpath by the roadway
    C   the gutter running down the side of the road
    D   the grass along the edge of the road

4. What reason did Tina give for **not** being interested in Mr Wheeler's advice?
    A   she wasn't old enough to go to school
    B   the traffic wardens told her when to cross the road
    C   her mother drove her to school
    D   she knew the crossing-the-road rules

5. Mick thought the best place to cross the street was
    A   in front of the school   B   at a pedestrian crossing
    C   from a verge   D   in a one-way street

6. According to the script which statement is CORRECT?
    A   The children saw Tina's mum drive down the street.
    B   Mr Wheeler gave his lesson at the school gate.
    C   The lights at the intersection were not working.
    D   It was safe to cross the street near the school.

7. Which option best describes how Mr Wheeler felt by the end of his lesson?
    A   he was pleased with himself
    B   he was embarrassed by the children
    C   he was unsure of his success
    D   he was content with what he had achieved

Lit Tip 9 – Improve your Literacy skills   **Proper nouns**
(Before you start check out **Lit Tip 8**.)

While a common noun names a person, place or thing a **proper noun** gets more specific. It gives the actual name of a person, place or thing. A proper noun always begins with a capital letter.
Examples: girl/Wendy, place/Tasmania, car/Holden

Draw a line under the nouns in this sentence that should start with a capital.
Before easter my brother ken took a jetstar flight to bribie island in queensland.
Write one proper noun for the common noun of place. _____

Understanding Year 3 Comprehension
A. Horsfield © Five Senses Education © W. Marlin

Rock Ringtail Possum

The rock ringtail possum is about the size of a small rabbit. Unlike other possums the rock ringtails prefer to live among rock piles, rather than in established trees. They do not have tails, legs or claws as long as other possums. Like other possums their tail is flexible. The tail is hairy at the base but almost bare at the tip.

They have dense woolly fur which can vary in colour from grey to a reddish-grey. They have a darker central strip along their back from their head to halfway down their back. It has white patches underneath its small, round ears and both above and below the eyes.

Like most other possums they are <u>nocturnal</u> and move about rocky outcrops that have wide cracks. They feed on flowers, fruits and leaves of small plants.

Rock ringtails are quite timid and do not move far from their rocky home when searching for ____(7)____ .

They are marsupials and like other possums they carry their young on their backs when they get too large for the pouch. They breed the whole year round giving birth to one youngster.

Rock ringtails are native to the Kimberley region of Western Australia.

Adapted from: http://en.wikipedia.org/wiki/Rock-haunting_ringtail_possum

Mammals from North Western Australia (What animal is that?) Carolyn Thompson-Dans

Department of Conservation Bush Books 2002

Understanding Descriptions

Circle a letter to answer questions 1 to 7.

1. The rock ringtail possum mainly lives
    - A   in rabbit burrows
    - B   on rocky outcrops
    - C   in established trees
    - D   near waterholes

2. Where are white patches located on rock ringtail possums?
    - A   along its back
    - B   on the tips of its ears
    - C   around its eyes
    - D   under its chin

3. Because it is timid the rock ringtail possum
    - A   has a pouch for its baby
    - B   eats flowers and leaves
    - C   breeds the whole year round
    - D   stays close to its home

4. Which statement is **not** correct?
    - A   Rock ringtail possums live in trees.
    - B   Rock ringtail possums carry their young on their backs.
    - C   Rock ringtail possums have a pouch.
    - D   Rock ringtail possums have bare tipped tails.

5. You read that possums are *nocturnal*.
    A *nocturnal* animal is one that
    - A   has one baby each year
    - B   does not have claws
    - C   lives amongst rocks
    - D   is active at night

6. Which of these words from the text is a proper noun? (Check out **Lit Tip 9**.)
    - A   halfway   B   marsupials   C   Kimberley   D   outcrops

7. A word has been deleted from the text.
    Which word would be best suited to the space (7)?
    - A   food   B   rocks   C   babies   D   rabbits

Lit Tip 10 – Improve your Literacy skills   **Synonyms**

A synonym is a word that means nearly the same as another word, for example,
shut is a synonym for *close*. Synonyms are words with *similar* meanings.
It is important to pick the best synonym for words in your writing.
Can you see differences in *beautiful, pretty, attractive, lovely,* and *stunning*?

1. Read: It was a *nice* day. A synonym for nice would be _____.
2. Draw a line to match these words with their synonym.

big	rowdy
sad	large
noisy	glum

rich	reply
clever	wealthy
answer	smart

Understanding Year 3 Comprehension
A. Horsfield © Five Senses Education © W. Marlin

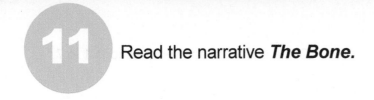

The Bone

Scruffy lay on his mat on the veranda chewing a large bone. "Mmm," he growled softly. It tasted good!

When he had had enough chewing and gnawing he took it across the back lawn to bury it in his secret hiding spot - in the soft <u>dirt</u> behind the garden shed.

Unfortunately he didn't see next-door's dog, Brutus watching him like a sneak from behind Mr Jacob's ute.

The next day when Scruffy went to dig up his bone it was gone. He thought he might have dug up the wrong spot so he dug another hole, then another hole, then another hole but no bone was found. All he had was a row of holes like postholes for a fence, along the back wall of the shed.

Just as he gave up he spotted a bit of dog hair caught on a small hole in the fence and he guessed what had happened! Brutus, Mr Jacob's little corgi had stolen his bone.

Scruffy was too big to fit through the hole in the fence but he did have a plan to get his bone back.

The next day he buried another bone but this time he spied Brutus watching him from near the back wheel of the ute. Brutus thought he was hidden but Scruffy could see his paws near the curve of the tyre.

Scruffy hoped his plan would work.

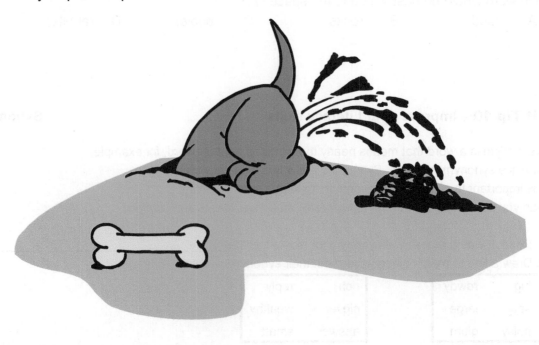

Understanding Narratives

Circle a letter or write an answer for questions 1 to 7.

1. Where was Brutus hiding?
   - A behind the garden shed
   - B under a mat on the veranda
   - C behind Mr Jacob's ute
   - D in the garden

2. Scruffy did **not** go after Brutus when he saw hair on the fence because he
   - A was afraid of Brutus
   - B couldn't get through the hole in the fence
   - C didn't know where Brutus might be hiding
   - D decided to find another bone

3. Scruffy buried his bone in the *dirt*.
   Which word is a synonym for *dirt* as used in the text? (Check **Lit Tip 10**.)
   - A grime
   - B mess
   - C ground
   - D filth

4. Brutus could best be described as
   - A clever and trustworthy
   - B sneaky and mean
   - C frightened and glum
   - D bold and friendly

5. Write the numbers 1 to 4 in the boxes to show the correct order in which events occurred in the narrative. The first one (1) has been done for you.

	Brutus watches Scruffy bury the bone
	Scruffy buries his bone in the dirt
	the buried bone disappears
1	Scruffy enjoys a bone on the back veranda

6. Which words from the text are an example of a simile?
   - A the curve of the tyre
   - B he spotted a bit of dog hair
   - C chewing and gnawing
   - D like postholes for a fence

7. When Scruffy discovered his bone was not where he had buried it he
   - A panicked looking for it
   - B attacked Brutus
   - C climbed through the fence
   - D hid behind the wheel of the ute

Lit Tip 11 – Improve your Literacy skills   Antonyms

An antonym is a word with an opposite meaning, for example: young - old.

1. Read: Rod came *first* in the race. An antonym for *first* would be _____.

2. Draw a line to match these words with their antonym.

fast	light
dark	quiet
noisy	slow

dead	false
true	ask
answer	alive

3. Sometimes a prefix can make an antonym: happy-<u>un</u>happy, able-<u>un</u>able

Use a prefix to make the antonym for *fair*. _____

Understanding Year 3 Comprehension
A. Horsfield © Five Senses Education © W. Marlin

Read the advertising flier *Taps for Tinies.*

Tracey picked up this flier at a community market.

Taps for Tinies

TAPS FOR TINIES

Children's Tap Classes

(ages 5 to 9 years)

Lessons commence on the first Friday of each school term.
Lessons start at 4 pm and run until 5 pm with a short 5-minute break.

All lessons are held in the Banksia State School gym.
It is <u>secure</u> and has an easy drop-off and pick-up point outside the gym.

Tap dancing is not only great exercise, but is wonderful for
coordination, rhythm - and is **FUN. It is exhilarating!**

Experienced teacher, Tanya "Twinkle Toes" Talbert has designed lessons for
beginner tappers as well as those who have had an introduction to tap dancing.

Tanya guarantees that every child will have
lots of **FUN** while learning the correct techniques and tap combinations.

Class numbers are limited and must be paid for before the first Friday of
each term. Cost per term is $120. No refunds after the third week.

NOTE: Tap dancing shoes can be provided for a short
period until parents obtain suitable shoes.

For more information contact Tanya:

twinkletoes@mynet.com.au (after 6 pm week days)

Understanding Persuasions

Circle a letter to answer questions 1 to 7.

1. Tanya Talbert holds her tap dance class lessons
    - A   at her private home
    - B   in the Banksia State School gym
    - C   in a school classroom
    - D   at the pick-up point outside the gym

2. Tap dance lessons are held
    - A   every Friday of each term between 4 pm and 5 pm
    - B   after the first Friday of each term between 4 pm and 5 pm
    - C   each Friday of each school term after 6 pm
    - D   on week days after 6 pm

3. The flier claims that tap dancing is exhilarating!
    The word *exhilarating* means
    - A   very exhausting
    - B   becoming dizzy
    - C   joyfully exciting
    - D   feeling anxious

4. If a child joins the class but does not have tap dance shoes they
    - A   cannot participate in a lesson
    - B   should dance bare-footed
    - C   buy shoes at the dance class
    - D   use loan shoes provided by the teacher

5. The best way to get more information on the tap dance classes is to
    - A   contact Tanya by email
    - B   talk to Tanya after 3 o'clock
    - C   enrol in the tap dance lessons
    - D   re-read the flier carefully

6. This flier is most likely meant to
    - A   explain what tap dancing is
    - B   report on the place where tap dance classes are held
    - C   describe how to do tap dance steps
    - D   persuade people to enrol in tap dance classes

7. The pick-up point outside the gym is described as being a secure place.
    As used in the flier which word is a synonym for *secure*?(Check **Lit Tip 10.**)
    - A   fixed   B   safe   C   locked   D   reliable

Lit Tip 12 – Improve your Literacy skills   **Ordinals (Ordinal numbers)**

Ordinals give the place of something in a series, such as first or second.
They can be written as words or a mixture of words and letters (abbreviations).
Examples: first-1st, second-2nd, third-3rd, fourth-4th, fifth-5th . . . tenth-10th
In most narrative writing ordinals are written as words.
When writing the date we do not include the letters, e.g. 8 May **not** 8th May.

Write these ordinal numbers the short way.
sixth _____, ninth _____, twenty-third _____, eleventh_____

Understanding Year 3 Comprehension
A. Horsfield © Five Senses Education © W. Marlin

Rhys

Rhys lived with his parents in a brick house in a big town. His father went to work everyday at a travel agent's office in the shopping centre. When Rhys left home for school his mother also went to work. She owned a health food shop in the main street. Rhys's parents were very <u>busy</u> people. They said they never had enough time to do all the things they wanted to do.

"There are not enough hours in a day," Rhys's father often said when he came home from work.

"Not enough days in the week," his mother would reply. Sometimes Rhys's father would have to go away. He would have to look at the places people might want to go to for holidays. On special trips he would take Rhys's mother. It was like a little holiday.

When that happened, Rhys went to stay with his retired grandparents in a small cottage by a quiet lake.

Rhys didn't mind when his parents went away because he enjoyed his grandparents's company and he loved staying with them. They seemed to have all the time in the world for walks along the shore, working in the garden or just sitting on their front verandah reading books and newspapers.

Better still they had time to listen to all he had to say. And in return they would tell him stories about interesting things and people. They never said that there was not enough time to do something.

Understanding Narratives

Circle a letter or write an answer for questions 1 to 7.

1. Where did Rhys's mother work?
    - A   in a health food shop
    - B   in a travel agent's office
    - C   in a shopping centre
    - D   in a garden

2. Rhys really liked staying with his grand parents because they
    - A   took him on holidays
    - B   lived by the shore of a lake
    - C   had time to talk and listen
    - D   went shopping at the shopping centre

3. Rhys's grandparents' home was near a
    - A   shopping centre
    - B   main street
    - C   store
    - D   lake

4. Which word in the text is a synonym for *vacation*? (Check **Lit Tip 10**.)

    Write your answer in the box. ☐

5. You read: *Rhys's parents were very <u>busy</u> people.*
    A *busy* person is a person who has
    - A   a lot of things to do
    - B   time to have a holiday
    - C   a job to go to each day
    - D   the time to read the newspaper

6. Any two words joined together are called compound words, e.g. newspaper is news + paper.
    Which of these words from the text is a compound word?
    - A   verandah
    - B   interesting
    - C   grandparents
    - D   happened

7. Which word best describes Rhys's grandparents?
    - A   strict   B   caring   C   lonely   D   busy

Lit Tip 13 – Improve your Literacy skills   **Writer or narrator?**

It is important to know the difference between the **writer** of a story and the **narrator**. The **writer** may also be called the **author**. It is the person who has their name on the front of the book. Charles Dickens wrote *A Christmas Carol*. He is the author.

Sometimes the author lets a character in the story tell the story. In *Treasure Island* a young boy (Jack Hawkins) is the story teller. He narrates the story as if it is his story but he is really only a character in the book. The narrator uses the pronoun *I* to relate the story (*I* went on board the ship.)
Check some of your books to see if any have a narrator.

Understanding Year 3 Comprehension
A. Horsfield © Five Senses Education © W. Marlin

14 Read the poem *Searching for Monsters* by Elaine Horsfield.

Searching for Monsters

I've never seen a monster
Though I know there's lots about
'Cause you see them advertised all over town.
And I'd really like to find one
Then I'd keep him as a pet.
A monster might be fun to have around.

Last week I went to buy one
Where they had a "Monster Sale"
But they must have sold them all the day before.
Because I hunted all around
And looked on all the shelves,
But I couldn't see a monster in that store.

I've looked around at "Monster Fetes"
And never seen a thing
That I would call a monster on the stalls.
I once went to the Easter Show
And bought a "Monster Bag",
But that just had some posters for my walls.

Today mum bought a ticket
In a raffle at our school,
That has a "Monster Hamper" as first prize.
And maybe if we win it,
I'll finally get to have

A monster, like the ones they advertise.

Elaine Horsfield

From: Alphabet Soup 2015

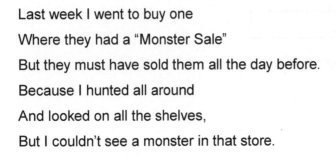

Understanding Poetry

Circle a letter or write an answer for questions 1 to 7.

1. The narrator believes monsters exist because
   (Forgotten who the narrator is? Check out **Lit Tip 13**.)
   - A   he has a picture of one on a poster
   - B   he saw some in a store
   - C   they are often given away as prizes
   - D   they are advertised all over town

2. How does the narrator react to monsters?
   - A   he would like to have one for a pet
   - B   he is frightened of them
   - C   he is not sure about trusting them
   - D   he thinks they should be treated with care

3. What was found in the monster bag from the Easter Show?
   - A   a raffle book   B   wall posters
   - C   a prize   D   show tickets

4. What reason did the narrator give for **not** finding a monster in the store?
   - A   he couldn't find one on the shelf
   - B   the store was about to close
   - C   they had all been sold
   - D   they were hidden from view

5. Pretend the narrator's mother won the Monster Hamper.
   When they had checked out the contents the narrator would most likely feel
   - A   disappointed   B   joyful
   - C   relaxed   D   pleased

6. The narrator finally hoped to find a monster to take home
   - A   at a monster sale   B   at a monster fete
   - C   in a monster bag   D   in a monster hamper

7. Which word rhymes with *store* in stanza (verse) 2?

   Write your answer in the box.

Lit Tip 14 – Improve your Literacy skills   Contractions

A contraction is two words made shorter by leaving out some letters and placing an apostrophe (')
where the letters have been omitted. The two words are squeezed together.
Example: *I'm* for *I am* and *who'll* for *who will*.

What are these words contractions for?

1. it's _____, you're _____, isn't _____, let's _____
2. A line from the poem: *Then I'd keep him as a pet.*

What is *I'd* short for? _____ Which letters have been left out? _____

Understanding Year 3 Comprehension
A. Horsfield © Five Senses Education © W. Marlin

The Mimic Octopus

Mimic type octopuses are capable of impersonating other creatures to avoid predators or become a <u>predator</u>. They have the unique ability of taking the shape of various objects and animals. They can change their skin colour and texture to blend in with their surroundings, such as algae covered rocks or nearby coral.

Many animals can imitate a different species to avoid or frighten predators, but the mimic octopus is the only one that can imitate a wide a range of shapes to avoid predators. It can twist body and tentacles into more than 15 different shapes, including snakes, lionfish, flatfish, jellyfish and stingrays.

The mimic octopus was first discovered in Indonesia in 1998. It was thought to only inhabit Indonesian islands until one was spotted near the Great Barrier Reef on a warm shallow sand flat near Lizard Island in June 2010.

As with all octopuses, the mimic octopus has eight tentacles, a mantle containing 3 hearts and other internal organs, and a siphon used for jet propulsion. The tentacles have two rows of suckers, each sucker having a touch sensor and can recognise certain chemicals, allowing the mimic effectively to feel and taste its food before it eats it. It lacks the sense of hearing.

Sources: http://en.wikipedia.org/wiki/Mimic_octopus

http://www.dive-the-world.com/creatures-mimic-octopus.php

Understanding Reports

1. Where was the mimic octopus first discovered?
   - A   Lizard Island
   - B   Great Barrier Reef
   - C   Indonesia
   - D   Australia

2. According to the text the mimic octopuses can take on the form of
   - A   snakes   B   starfish   C   turtles   D   crabs

3. According to the text which statement is CORRECT?
   The mimic octopus
   - A   is not hunted by predators
   - B   can mimic a wide variety of sea creatures
   - C   has six tentacles
   - D   prefers cool seawater

4. Which fact about the mimic octopus is TRUE?
   - A   it moves itself along using its tentacles
   - B   it has a single row of suckers on its tentacles
   - C   it has three hearts
   - D   it is very good at hearing

5. The mimic octopus is described as a *predator* in paragraph 1.
   A *predator* is an animal that
   - A   kills another animal for food
   - B   defends itself against other animals
   - C   finds places to hide from other animals
   - D   becomes the food for another animal

6. Paragraph 1 states that mimic octopuses are *able to change their skin colour and texture to blend in with their surroundings.*
   This could best be described as
   - A   cunning   B   camouflage   C   deceit   D   imitation

7. According to the text how many different forms can the mimic octopus make?

   Write your answer on the line._____

Lit Tip 15 – Improve your Literacy skills   **Singular or plural?**

Singular refers to one noun. **Plural** refers to more than one noun.
Example: One boy but many boys. For most plural nouns you add s or es.
Compare these singular and plural nouns: pig/pigs, box/boxes, witch/witches
What is the plural of these? (It helps to say the words aloud.)

fox _____, ghost _____, bite _____, quiz _____

What is the singular of these?

sixes _____, ashes _____, cakes _____, waltzes _____
From the text.
What is the plural of: octopus? _____ , tentacle _____

Understanding Year 3 Comprehension
A. Horsfield © Five Senses Education © W. Marlin

What are Mangroves?

Mangrove trees live between the land and the sea. They are unlike any other plant. They continue to grow as the water changes from fresh to salt and from salt to fresh.

Mangroves grow in salty mud on the edge of the sea. There are many different types.

One mangrove tree has roots that make a maze of arches that grow off its trunk. This helps it to live in changes of water levels.

The white mangrove has cable roots growing out from the trunk. Pencil like roots then poke up through the mud.

Another mangrove has roots like upright slabs of woods (**buttresses**) growing around the trunk.

Wading through mangroves is difficult! They are smelly. The trees are a tangle of trunks and full of insects, but they are worth saving.

Mangroves provide a source of fish and food for other sea animals. The rotting leaves are food for crabs. Bigger fish visit the mangroves to eat the mud crabs.

They are also the home of young sea animals, such as oysters, prawns and fish, that later leave the 'nursery' for life in deeper water.

Mangroves protect the coastline. Their roots hold the muddy soil in place and stop it being eroded. Roots trap rooting leaves and branches, which help to make more soil.

Mangrove swamps give shelter to many plants, sea animals and birds. The mudskipper is a small fish that uses its fins like legs. It climbs up mangrove roots to escape danger.

Mangroves are amazing trees that should be saved.

Adapted from: www.island-spirit.org/uploads/medialibrary/2012/04/mangroves.pdf

http://en.wikipedia.org/wiki/Mudskipper

Understanding Explanations

Circle a letter to answer questions 1 to 7.

1. What is special about mangroves?
   - A   they survive in mud
   - B   they are a home for many animals
   - C   their roots form great tangles
   - D   they can live in both fresh water and salt water

2. The roots of the mangroves are important in that they
   - A   stop people entering swamps
   - B   have many interesting root shapes
   - C   prevent erosion along the coast
   - D   are fun places to explore

3. Rotting mangrove leaves are a source of food for
   - A   mudskippers   B   mud crabs   C   oysters   D   prawns

4. Which of these statements from the text expresses an OPINION of the writer?
   - A   Mangroves are amazing trees that should be saved.
   - B   The rotting leaves are food for crabs.
   - C   The white mangrove has cable roots growing out from the trunk.
   - D   Mangroves grow in salty mud on the edge of the sea.

5. What does the mudskipper do to avoid danger?
   - A   it hides among the mangrove roots
   - B   it swims out to deeper water
   - C   it burrows into the mud
   - D   it crawls up mangrove roots

6. Which statement best sums up how the writer feels about mangroves?
   - A   Mangroves need to be cleared of nasty creatures.
   - B   Mangroves are dangerous places for animals.
   - C   Mangroves are a valuable part of the environment.
   - D   Mangroves are smelly places and should be cleared.

7. The text in this article is most likely
   - A   a reference book entry on trees
   - B   part of an adventure story
   - C   instructions on mangrove safety
   - D   a recount of a walk through mangroves

Lit Tip 16 – Improve your Literacy skills   Odd plurals

In **Lit Tip 15** you were told that most plural nouns end in *s* or *es*.
Some common exceptions: child/children, goose/geese. ox/oxen

What is the plural of: tooth _____, man _____, mouse _____
For some nouns the singular and plural are the same.
Examples: sheep, deer, jellyfish, salmon, offspring, moose
Some words ending with *f* or *fe* ending have their own rule: life/lives, wolf/wolves

Understanding Year 3 Comprehension
A. Horsfield © Five Senses Education © W. Marlin

(Meg had to write about something she would like to see changed.)

Kids in Supermarkets

Supermarkets are not the place for young children. Most kids do not know how to behave and are very annoying to other shoppers. I am not referring to babies, but kids that can walk - and run!

Firstly, there are the screamers - kids that use high-pitched screams and can be heard all over the supermarket. Nothing pleases them. If they sit in the trolley they scream to get out. If they are walking they scream for a ride! Never satisfied. Do the parents do anything? No! These kids should be banned from supermarkets.

Secondly there are the chasers. These kids think supermarkets are a great place to play chasing. They don't worry about interrupting people trying to shop. The worse chasers are the ones who <u>taunt</u> each other. Do the parents do anything? No!

Thirdly there are the destroyers. Have you ever seen kids pulling things off shelves and just leaving them on the floor? Or they open packets or eat small bits of fruit. Do the parents do anything? No!

Then there are the badgers - the kids that whine from the moment they enter the supermarket to the time they finally exit the checkout. Always loudly nagging their parents to buy them something! Do the parents do anything? Yes! They give in. Anything for a break from the whinging kid! Not a good lesson for the kid.

I believe young children should be banned from supermarkets or make the supermarket have a child-minding room so that people can shop in ____(7)____!

Understanding Opinions

Circle a letter to answer questions 1 to 7.

1. How does Meg feel about young children in supermarkets?
   - A   Meg strongly disapproves of young children in supermarkets.
   - B   Meg doesn't worry about young children in supermarkets.
   - C   Meg has some interest in allowing young children in supermarkets.
   - D   Meg takes no notice of young children in supermarkets.

2. How do some parents react to a whinging child?
   - A   they let them run in the supermarket aisles
   - B   they buy them whatever they want
   - C   they ignore them
   - D   they put them in a child-minding room

3. In paragraph 3 Meg talks about children who taunt each other
   What would be a suitable synonym for *taunt*? (Check **Lit Tip 10**.)
   - A   call   B   hurt   C   haunt   D   tease

4. Which group of children does Meg actually say should be banned from supermarkets?
   - A   those with high-pitched screams   B   young babies
   - C   kids that pester their parents   D   those who play chasings

5. What does Meg say supermarkets could do to make shopping more pleasant?
   - A   encourage parents to buy whatever their children want
   - B   set up child-minding rooms
   - C   ban parents with babies from the supermarket
   - D   encourage kids to ride in the trolleys

6. Meg feels that supermarket shopping is
   - A   an enjoyable outing   B   a worthwhile venture
   - C   an unpleasant experience   D   a complicated task

7. The last word has been deleted from the text.
   Which word would be best suited to the space (7)?
   - A   company   B   hope   C   peace   D   warmth

Understanding Year 3 Comprehension
A. Horsfield © Five Senses Education © W. Marlin

Frozen Honeycomb Slice

This creamy frozen honeycomb slice is a delicious combination of malty biscuits, creamy ice cream and crunchy honeycomb. Kids will love making it.

Ingredients:

- 1 packet (250g) Malt 'O' Milk biscuits
- 600mL thickened cream
- 1 tin (395g) condensed milk
- 1 packet (400g) chocolate coated honeycomb

Preparation Time: 20 minutes + 3 hours freezing time

Cooking Time: 0 mins

Number of serves: 16

Method:

Step 1. Take a baking tray a bit larger than an A4 school worksheet and line with baking paper. Place malt biscuits, face side up to cover the entire base.

Step 2. Chop honeycomb roughly with a knife. If the kids are making this slice then they can put the honeycomb in a resealable bag and crush with a rolling pin.

Step 3. In a mixing bowl, whip the cream until thick and add the condensed milk and mix until just combined. Add half of the honeycomb to the cream mixture and stir until combined.

Step 4. Pour the mixture into the tray over the biscuits and smooth the top. Sprinkle the remaining honeycomb chips over the top. Freeze for 3 hours or until set. Slice into squares and serve chilled.

Adapted from: http://www.kidspot.com.au/best-recipes/Kids-cooking+5/Frozen-honeycomb-slice-recipe+5595.htm

Understanding Procedures

Circle a letter or write an answer for questions 1 to 7.

1. Which step in the recipe are the instructions for mixing the cream, condensed milk and some of the honeycomb pieces?

   A   Step 1   B   Step 2   C   Step 3   D   Step 4

2. What would the honeycomb slice most likely taste like?

   A   smooth   B   crunchy   C   brittle   D   tough

3. How many servings does this recipe for honeycomb slice make?

   A   2   B   4   C   8   D   16

4. How long does it take to cook the honeycomb slice?

   A   no cooking required
   B   about 16 minutes
   C   20 minutes
   D   3 hours

5. Write the numbers 1 to 4 in the boxes to show the correct order for the first steps in this procedure. The first one (1) has been done for you.

	cover the baking paper with biscuits
	line the tray base with baking paper
	crush the honeycomb
1	collect the ingredients

6. Which ingredient is not required when making honeycomb slice?

   A   condensed milk   B   malt biscuits
   C   thickened cream   D   sugar

7. It is suggested for children they should prepare the honeycomb by

   A   breaking it up with their hands
   B   mixing it up in a mixing bowl
   C   crushing it in a plastic bag using a rolling pin
   D   chopping it up roughly with a knife

Lit Tip 18 – Improve your Literacy skills　　　　**Better words than *got***

Got is the past tense for get. *Got* does not improve your writing.
Compare these two examples. Tim (*got, earned*) $2 for mowing the lawn.
Earned has a lot more meaning.

Underline the word you think best completes these sentences.
1. Ann (*got, fetched, retrieved*) the mail from the letterbox.
2. The baby (*got, grabbed, took*) hold of the spoon.
3. Add a good *got* word for the space. Barney _____ off the fallen tree.
Remember, it's not just that *get* and *got* are over-used but more precise words engage the reader.

Understanding Year 3 Comprehension
A. Horsfield © Five Senses Education © W. Marlin

Old Mike

It's hard to imagine what Old Mike really looked like. He had a floppy hat that he had woven himself on rainy nights. It was made from the fibre of cabbage tree palm. A few corks dangled from the brim to keep summer flies from landing. It was interesting that his hat, his beard and the end of his nose were about all you would ever see of Old Mike's face.

Mike had lived in the bush with timber and horses since boyhood. His skin was more a tanned <u>hide</u> than anything else. It was impossible to tell Mike's age. His appearance was that of a grand old man but he was no more than fifty years.

He was strong. Strong as any bullock in a bullock team he would say of himself. Of course he was human, and he dreamed the dreams of old men who had seen changes in the bush. Now the bullock teams had all but vanished.

On any rainy evening because there was time, and a break from the hard work of day-to-day living in the bush with his bullock teams, he would sit silently before his smoky log fire and dream. He didn't dream of wealth. He didn't dream of a more comfortable hut or even company. He dreamed of the way things were, when life was simpler.

To him those days were the good old days.

Understanding Descriptions

Circle a letter to answer questions 1 to 7.

1. What feature about Old Mike does the writer find most interesting?
   - A   the way his face was hidden   B   the colour of his skin
   - C   the way he spent his nights   D   the age of the man

2. Which hat was Old Mike most likely to wear?

   A   B   C   D

3. What is meant by the word *hide* as used in paragraph 2?
   - A   put out of sight   B   leathery skin
   - C   not worried by insults   D   a secret place to watch events

4. Old Mike's life had been
   - A   hard but satisfying   B   peaceful but miserable
   - C   boring and tragic   D   cheerful and exciting

5. What work did Old Mike do when he was younger?
   - A   built cabins in the bush
   - B   cut firewood
   - C   made hats from cabbage tree palms
   - D   drove bullock teams

6. Which option is an example of a simile?
   - A   the bullock teams had all but vanished
   - B   he dreamed of the way things were
   - C   Mike had lived in the bush
   - D   strong as any bullock in a bullock team

7. How does the writer feel about Old Mike?
   - A   the writer feels sorry for him
   - B   the writer feels respect for him
   - C   the writer feels worried about him
   - D   the writer feels excited for him

Lit Tip 19 – Improve your Literacy skills   **Possession by on**

The apostrophe s ('s) is used to show some<u>one</u> or some<u>thing</u> has ownership.

Examples: *Bob's books* could have been written as the *books of Bob*.

         a *truck's wheels* could have been written as *the wheels of a truck*

Show ownership by using an apostrophe s ('s).

1. a bark of the dog _____   2. a smile of Sue _____

3. the bag of the lady _____   4. the hat of the man _____

5. the fee of Dr Low _____   6. the ears of a fox _____

Understanding Year 3 Comprehension
A. Horsfield © Five Senses Education © W. Marlin

What is a Heteronym

A *heteronym* is a word having the same spelling as another word, but a different sound and meaning. (You don't have to remember that word!)

Example:

1. Even camels need water in a <u>desert</u>.

2. It is being disloyal to <u>desert</u> your friends.

In English there are quite a few.

- In NSW there is a town called Scone which rhymes with bone. However, the *scone* you eat with jam and cream rhymes with Don.

- Golfers can be seen *putting* on greens but librarians are seen *putting* books on shelves.

- Jack always does his homework. AND There were two *does* and a buck in my uncle's rabbit hutch.

- The wind whistles through the trees. AND *Wind* the string up into a ball.

- *Excuse* me. I sit here! AND What is your *excuse* this time?

There are number of heteronyms where the pronunciation varies in speech according to whether the word is used as a verb (action words) or as a noun (naming words) or adjective (describing words).

Some examples include:

- It was at that <u>min</u>ute(noun) we saw a mi<u>nute</u> (adjective) light on the hill.

- Tell the <u>Pol</u>ish (adjective) driver to po<u>lish</u> (verb) the car.

Some single syllable words follow a similar pattern

- I have a *bow* (noun) and arrow. AND Actors *bow* (verb) to their audience.

- You can read (verb, present tense) this book? AND I have *read* (verb, past tense) that magazine.

The trick with heteronyms is to get the pronunciation right.

Adapted from: http://www.fun-with-words.com/nym_heteronyms.html

http://richard.tangle-wood.co.uk/heteronym.html

Understanding Explanations

Circle a letter or write an answer for questions 1 to 7.

1. Read this sentence.
   The fast growing vine will *wind* itself through the branches of the tree!
   What does *wind* mean in this sentence?
   - A   twisting up around parts of the tree
   - B   completely covering
   - C   turning a key or handle in a mechanical device
   - D   a strong current of air

2. The trick with heteronyms is to get (Tick a box.)

   A   the spelling right ☐   B   the pronunciation right ☐

3. Look at this sentence. Which underlined word is the adjective?
   We *live* by the lake in a house with a faulty *live* wire.
   A   B

4. Look at this sentence. *I can row a boat*.
   Which word does *row* rhyme with in this sentence?
   - A   cow   B   too   C   now   D   go

5. What is the meaning of *desert* as used in Example 1 in the first paragraph?
   - A   leave a person in a dangerous place
   - B   a sweet dish that completes a meal
   - C   a large dry area of little rainfall
   - D   go from a place without permission

6. Who is most likely to say: I saw Bev *putting* a ball into a hole in the grass.
   - A   a builder   B   a gardener
   - C   a librarian   D   a golfer

7. Look at this sentence. There was a *tear* in the sheet.
   Which word does *tear* rhyme with in this sentence?
   - A   wear   B   here   C   beer   D   fear

Lit Tip 20 – Improve your Literacy skills   **More on heteronyms**

Can you use these words in sentences to show two different meanings.
Remember you pronounce them differently.

lead _____

lead _____

Read these sentences and carefully pronounce the underline words.

When the fire was <u>close</u> to town the firemen had to <u>close</u> the roads.
The nurse <u>wound</u> a bandage around the head <u>wound</u>.
A female pig is a <u>sow</u>. The gardener will <u>sow</u> seeds in spring.
The weather was <u>windy</u> as we walked along the <u>windy</u> track.

Understanding Year 3 Comprehension
A. Horsfield © Five Senses Education © W. Marlin

Marsupial Lion

An almost complete skeleton of the extinct marsupial lion (*Thylacoleo carnifex*) was discovered in the Nullarbor Caves in Western Australia. It is believed the beast may have fallen into the caves purely by accident, perhaps when hunting or lured by the scent of ___(7)___. Imagine a predator the size of a leopard, but built like a bear. It was capable of sitting up like a kangaroo. It had huge claws for ripping apart its prey. It was able to climb trees because it has thumbs that face and can touch the other fingers on the same hand. For its size the marsupial lion had a bite more powerful than any known mammal living or extinct.

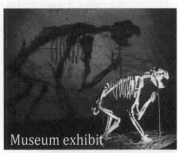

Museum exhibit

What Scientists Can Tell from Teeth

Thylacoleo had no canines (pointed teeth) in the lower jaw, and only small, almost useless canines in the upper jaw. The inner incisors (cutting teeth) however were larger in relation to the other teeth and were like the incisors of a rodent.

The molars or back teeth were used for grinding plant material. All were very small except one. One molar however had evolved into an enormous bolt-like cutting device, enabling the marsupial lion to slice through flesh with ease. It would have mainly fed on flesh as it did not have teeth capable of cracking bones.

Most of Australia's larger extinct marsupials ate plant matter.

Adapted from: http://en.wikipedia.org/wiki/Thylacoleo

http://www.museum.wa.gov.au/cave/beasts-nullarbor

Understanding Reports

Circle a letter or write an answer for questions 1 to 7.

1. The build of the marsupial lion could be compared to that of a

   A   bear   B   rodent   C   lion   D   kangaroo

2. The marsupial lion had a number of different teeth.
   Its incisors were used to

   A   rip flesh apart   B   cut through flesh
   C   grind bones   D   crack bones

3. What was special about the thumbs of the marsupial lion?

   A   they were longer than its fingers
   B   they were on opposite sides of its palm
   C   they allowed the lion to climb trees
   D   they helped in the collecting of plant food

4. Why do scientists find teeth important?
   The teeth show

   A   what and how the animal ate
   B   how the animal protected itself
   C   the age of the animal when it died
   D   why the animal became extinct

5. The reason (*Thylacoleo carniflex*) is in italics and brackets is because it

   A   is a difficult word to pronounce
   B   is the scientific name for the marsupial lion
   C   shows that the information is correct
   D   helps readers to understand the animal

6. How did the marsupial lion differ from most other Australian marsupials?

   A   it could climb trees   B   it has become extinct
   C   it could sit up on its back legs   D   it was a flesh eater

7. A word has been deleted from the text.
   Which word would be best suited to the space (7)?

   A   water   B   plants   C   food   D   leopards

Lit Tip 21 – Improve your Literacy skills   **Possession by many**

(Check out **Lit Tip 19**)
The s apostrophe (s') shows possession by two or more persons or things.
Examples: *the girls' noses could have been written as the noses of the girls*
            the foxes' howls could have been written as the howls of foxes

What is the plural of: baby _____, witch _____, box _____

To show ownership we write: babie<u>s</u>' food, witch<u>es</u>' hats, box<u>es</u>' lids

The apostrophe comes after the *s* (s').

Write the correct word in the space to show ownership by more than one.

(boy) _____ party, (parent) _____ home, (baby) _____ mother

Understanding Year 3 Comprehension
A. Horsfield © Five Senses Education © W. Marlin

Crocodile

Some people have puppies or birds that talk

Kittens that make you smile.

At our place we don't have any of those –

We just have a crocodile.

He's not really a pet. He lives in the creek,

But every once in a while

He wanders up to our back fence -

This curious crocodile.

One evening we sat on the deck, with no thought

Of a scaly grey reptile.

Then we saw the shape behind the fence -

A great big crocodile!

He slowly yawned and blinked his eyes,

And gave us a friendly smile,

Then he <u>shuffled</u> down into the creek –

Our resident crocodile!

Elaine Horsfield 2015

Understanding Poetry

Circle a letter or write an answer for questions 1 to 7.

1. What pet does the narrator of this poem say they have at their place?
   - A bird
   - B puppy
   - C kitten
   - D crocodile

2. Where was the crocodile often seen?
   - A up the creek
   - B at the back fence
   - C under the water
   - D on the back deck

3. Give two words from the poem that rhyme with crocodile.

   1. _____ , 2. _____

4. Which line from the poem would be most suitable for this drawing?
   - A Then we saw the shape behind the fence
   - B At our place we don't have any of those
   - C Some people have puppies or birds that talk
   - D Then he slithered down into the creek

5. The crocodile *shuffled* down into the creek.
   Shuffled means the crocodile
   - A marched boldly back into the creek
   - B hurried quickly back into the creek
   - C lumbered slowly back into the creek
   - D sneaked silently back into the creek

6. When the crocodile saw people on the back deck it
   - A got ready to attack
   - B showed little interest
   - C felt threatened
   - D decided to be friendly

7. The crocodile could best be described as
   - A neighbourly   B timid   C cunning   D dangerous

Lit Tip 22 – Improve your Literacy skills   **Using commas in lists**

Commas (,) are used to show pauses in text and to separate items in lists.
Examples: There are trucks, cars, vans and bikes at the show.
You will notice there is **no** comma after vans as it is followed by *and*.
Yellow, blue or red cakes are not for sale!
There is **no** comma after *blue* which is followed by *or*.

Add commas to these sentences.
1. Dogs cats pigs sheep and horses live on our farm.
2. We have cups glasses plates and napkins for the picnic.
3. In my class there are boys and girls.

Understanding Year 3 Comprehension
A. Horsfield © Five Senses Education © W. Marlin

Read the film review *Paddington.*

Paddington

Paddington is based on the children's book by Michael Bond, A Bear Called Paddington. The orphan bear had lived with his aunt and uncle in a rainforest in Peru. After a deadly earthquake destroys his home and kills his uncle, Paddington <u>stows away</u> on a ship bound for London. All he has on his lonely sea voyage is his red hat, a beat-up suitcase and multiple jars of marmalade. In London he hopes that someone will help him.

Photo: A Horsfield

Who will help Paddington? The Brown family, after some hesitation, welcome him into their home.

For all the misfortunes there is little that is upsetting in the film. Misfortunes are treated openly without dwelling on the distress.

In London Paddington gets into some dangerous mischief, which will delight and excite most kids. His exploits include sliding quickly down bannisters, flooding a bathroom, giving chase to a pickpocket, and finally being kidnapped by the scheming taxidermist (a person that stuffs animal skins for displays), Millicent Clyde (played by Nicole Kidman).

The Browns' aunt helps rescue Paddington by sharing a bottle of whisky with a security guard to distract him. The language is in no way offensive.

Paddington is very sweet, polite, and good intentioned but a little naive at times. The Brown family is typically English.

Paddington is a charming and amusing film.

David Alan 2015

Rated: GP
Suitable for families
Running time: 96 minutes
Score: ★ ★ ★ ★ ☆

Reference: *Paddington* Michael Bond HarperCollin's Children's Books 2007

Understanding Film Reviews

Circle a letter or write an answer for questions 1 to 7.

1. Who did Paddington live with in the rainforest?
   - A   the Brown family
   - B   his aunt and uncle
   - C   Millicent Clyde
   - D   Nicole Kidman

2. Which bear is most like Paddington?

A

B

C

D

3. In which country did Paddington live before he went to London?

   Write your answer in the box.

4. Who wrote this review?
   - A   David Alan
   - B   Millicent Clyde
   - C   Michael Bond
   - D   the Brown family

5. Which option best describes the film reviewer's opinion of the movie?
   - A   the film was ruined by bad language
   - B   it was disappointing
   - C   it was a very suitable family film
   - D   the film was uninteresting

6. Paddington is described as being a *little* <u>naive</u> at times.
   A *naive* person is one who
   - A   tries to be well behaved
   - B   is often unaware of problems
   - C   puts people in danger
   - D   plays tricks that are harmless

7. Which words have a similar meaning to *stows away* as used in the first paragraph?
   - A   gets a cabin
   - B   travels secretly
   - C   finds a job
   - D   sails off

Lit Tip 23 – Improve your Literacy skills   **Affixes**

Many English words are formed by adding affixes to them.

An **affix** is a group of letters added to a base word that changes its meaning in some way.

Example: <u>re</u>turn<u>ed</u>. The base word is *turn*.

The *re* means again. The *ed* changes the word to past tense.

Affixes can be more than two letters: <u>mid</u>field, pest<u>icide</u>.

1. Underline the base word in these: lovely, discover, preserve, reading

2. Underline the affixes in these: recovered, tricycles, unhelpful, hopelessness

Understanding Year 3 Comprehension
A. Horsfield © Five Senses Education © W. Marlin

Ginga

In the beginning of creation Ginga was also a man.

One day when he was sleeping near a billabong with his back to the campfire his back suddenly caught alight. He dashed into the water.

The fire and the water formed great blisters on his back. Ginga turned himself into a saltwater crocodile. His ragged, bumpy body can still be seen as he emerges from the water and sleeps along the banks of rivers and billabongs.

The giant crocodile Ginga also helped make the landform around Kakadu Park (Northern Territory), when he carved his way through the rocks to get to a coastal river. After completing his work he did not disappear but turned himself into a rocky ridge which still shows his lumpy back. The place is called Djirringbal.

It is believed his wide snout allowed him to form the landscape. It is also his wide snout that distinguishers him from his freshwater cousin.

Ginga is <u>at home</u> during the monsoon season. When the monsoon rains arrive he may head from costal swamps to far inland creeks and billabongs. Ginga is often seen feeding on wild geese stranded by rising waters. This is a time when the grasslands are flooded and food is <u>plentiful</u>.

Adapted from information available in the Kakadu National Park.

Understanding Legends

Circle a letter to answer questions 1 to 7.

1. In the beginning Ginga was a
   - A giant rock
   - B wild goose
   - C crocodile
   - D man

2. How did Ginga get a lumpy back?
   - A it happened as he made his way through rocks
   - B it resulted from scars he got while hunting
   - C it was blistered by fire and water
   - D it came from staying on a rocky ridge

3. When the monsoon season starts Ginga, the crocodile, heads for
   - A inland billabongs
   - B coastal streams
   - C rocky ridges
   - D a place called Djirringbal

4. Why did Ginga, as a man, jump into the water?
   - A he was trying to scare the crocodile
   - B he was running away from a crocodile
   - C he was trying to catch wild geese
   - D he burnt his back while sleeping by a campfire

5. This legend is meant to
   - A warn people about sleeping too close to fires
   - B explain why the crocodile has a rough back
   - C describe what the rocky ridges look like
   - D persuade people not to swim in billabongs

6. The last paragraph states: Ginga is <u>at home</u> during the monsoon season.
   What does *at home* mean in this sentence?
   - A Ginga is not going anywhere.
   - B Ginga is ready for visitors.
   - C Ginga has a place to live.
   - D Ginga is comfortable and relaxed.

7. Which word has a similar meaning to *plentiful* as used in the last sentence?
   - A nearby
   - B abundant
   - C available
   - D reliable

Lit Tip 24 – Improve your Literacy skills   Prefixes
(Check out **Lit Tip 23**.)

A **prefix** is placed at the start of a word. It changes the meaning in some way.

Some common prefixes and their meaning: pre/before, anti/against, ex/out

Prefixes may have more than one meaning. *Pro* can mean forward as in <u>pro</u>pel or it can mean before a certain time/place, as in <u>pro</u>posal.

Two different prefixes may have a similar meaning. Compare: <u>im</u>possible and <u>un</u>happy. The prefixes *un* and *im* can mean not.

A word can take several prefixes.
Add different prefixes to:_____cover, _____cover, _____cover

Understanding Year 3 Comprehension
A. Horsfield © Five Senses Education © W. Marlin

Read the recount **Growing Seeds.**

Growing Seeds

We had a science project with Ms Persson on plants. She said we should watch bean seeds grow, especially the roots. We would need a plant viewer. It would be a 3P class project.

Ms Persson cut the top off a large, white plastic milk bottle. She then removed one side. All that was left were three sides and the base.

Peter found a flat piece of clear plastic. It was rectangular in shape. This was taped firmly to the open front of the milk bottle. This meant we had a clear view into our milk bottle.

Trung filled the container with potting mix. He sprinkled some water onto it to make it damp.

Max planted three bean seeds in the soil close to the clear plastic viewer.

Because roots grow in darkness Ms Persson placed a small cardboard box over over our project. She then put it all into a cupboard at the back of the room.

After a week we took it out and removed the cardboard box. The seeds had sprouted tiny leaves. Through the viewer we could see the white thin roots growing down the inside.

Because plants need sunlight Fiona put the container near a window and Max sprinkled water on the beans each morning.

Last week we planted our seeds in the school garden.

Adapted from: http://www.kidsgardening.org/node/96821, https://books.google.com.au/books?isbn=1420680722(Jane Baker, Lesson 9)www.pinterest.com/ebrooke81/seedplant-lesson-plans/.

Understanding Recounts

Circle a letter for questions 1 to 7.

1. This recount tells how the class made a plant viewer
   - A   that only lasted for a week
   - B   using a glass bottle
   - C   that didn't work in the dark
   - D   in the order that they did things

2. Who put the plant viewer on the windowsill?
   - A   Trung
   - B   Ms Persson
   - C   Fiona
   - D   Max

3. What do the new roots of beans look like?
   They are
   - A   green and short
   - B   dark and long
   - C   bright and shiny
   - D   thin and white

4. The cut-out front of the plastic milk bottle was covered in clear plastic to
   - A   stop the seeds from falling out
   - B   allow students see how roots grow
   - C   let the sunlight in
   - D   check that the soil was damp

5. The experiment was kept in the a cupboard for a week so that the
   - A   students couldn't see what was happening
   - B   class could get on with their schoolwork
   - C   seeds could grow naturally in the dark
   - D   sunlight would not spoil the experiment

6. From the last sentence you know that
   - A   nothing was learned from the experiment
   - B   the plants had grown successfully
   - C   there was a mess to clean up
   - D   the leaves fell off the plants

7. Another suitable title for the text would be
   - A   3P's class project
   - B   Three bean seeds
   - C   Watering plants
   - D   Ms Persson's plants

Lit Tip 25 – Improve your Literacy skills   Short form for month names

For most months we can write them in a shortened form with three letters.
There is a stop after the short form.

Jan.	January	May	(no change)	Sept.	September
Feb.	February	June	(no change)	Oct.	October
Mar.	March	July	(no change)	Nov.	November
Apr.	April	Aug.	August	Dec.	December

Which month is shortened to 4 letters? _____

Understanding Year 3 Comprehension
A. Horsfield © Five Senses Education © W. Marlin

Types of Whistles

Many centuries ago night watchmen in Ancient China blew into the tops of acorns to warn towns of invaders.

Many types of whistles exist. There are the small mouth blown whistles with various uses from toys to hunting whistles mimicking bird calls. Whistles are used officially by the police, sailors (bosun's pipe), and the military.

Types of policemen's whistles

Pea whistles are important in sporting events. Children often use pea whistles as a toy music instrument. Pea whistles have been used in jazz bands.

Then there are much larger steam or air pressure whistles used on steam trains, ships and in factories.

Although almost all whistles have some musical character, whistles are not considered musical instruments since they cannot be played tunefully, unless their purpose is to provide a very shrilled sound.

However, musical whistles exist, including tin whistles (sometimes called penny whistles) as well as the calliope which is an arrangement of steam whistles.

There is a whistle used to give <u>commands</u> to working sheepdogs. It can emit almost any tone the shepherd wishes to give different commands. It is known as a shepherd's whistle. Australian farmers use their mouth for whistling commands.

Bosun's pipe

Sources: http://en.wikipedia.org/wiki/Whistle

http://www.wikipedia.or.ke/index.php/Whistle

Understanding Explanations

1. According to the text the sound made by most whistles is caused by
   - A   steam pressure
   - B   air forced through a hole
   - C   a pea in the whistle's structure
   - D   blowing into acorns

2. What is a *calliope*?
   - A   a set of whistles worked by steam
   - B   a policeman's whistle
   - C   a whistle used in a jazz band
   - D   a type of pea whistle

3. Whistles are official communication for
   - A   children's playing games
   - B   bands needing shrilled sounds
   - C   members of the military
   - D   sheep dog handlers

4. The writer of this text most likely intended this writing to be
   - A   valuable
   - B   inspiring
   - C   amusing
   - D   informative

5. Where would you most likely hear a steam whistle?
   - A   near a factory
   - B   in a police station
   - C   at a children's party
   - D   during a jazz band number

6. According to the text which statement about whistles is CORRECT?
   - A   All whistles use mouth blowing to make sounds.
   - B   Whistles are a modern invention.
   - C   Australian farmers use their mouth to whistle instructions to dogs.
   - D   Whistles are not used in the making of music.

7. In the last paragraph you read whistles are used *to give <u>commands</u>*.
   Which of these words could replace *commands*?
   - A   help
   - B   rules
   - C   requests
   - D   orders

Lit Tip 26 – Improve your Literacy skills　　　　　　　　　　　**Suffixes**

(Check out **Lit Tip 23 and 24**.)

A **suffix** is attached to the end of a word. It changes its meaning in some way.
Some common suffixes and their meaning: *s*/makes plural nouns, *ful*/full of.
dom/a place (kingdom), *less*/without (shoeless), *est*/most (quickest)
Suffixes can have more than one meaning: The suffix *er* can tell what a person does (paint/painter). It can give a comparison (fast/fast<u>er</u>).
A word can have more than one suffix.

Add different suffixes to: care _____, care _____, care _____

Understanding Year 3 Comprehension
A. Horsfield © Five Senses Education © W. Marlin

The Leaning Tower of Pisa

The Leaning Tower of Pisa is a freestanding circular bell tower of eight floors for the cathedral city of Pisa, Italy. The tower started to lean during construction because the foundation was built on soft ground. The lean became worse as construction continued over several decades.

The bottom storey has 15 marble arches. Each of the next six storeys contains 30 arches that surround the tower. The seven bells are located on the eighth floor.

Time Line

1173 - construction begins

1178 - construction stops at the second floor because the tower began to lean

1276 - (about) construction recommenced but stopped at the sixth floor

1284 - construction stopped because of war

1350 - 1372 tower was completed

1920s - the foundations of the tower were injected with cement that helped to stabilize the tower

1987 - the tower was given World Heritage listing

1989 - 2001 tower closed for restoration work. It was stabilized and the lean was partially fixed.

2008 - engineers claim the Tower had stopped moving. (The first time in its history that the Tower stopped slowly leaning further to one side.)

Work on the construction continued for over 800 years but there were many stops and starts.

Should the tower be straightened? What do you think?

Sources: http://www.softschools.com/facts/wonders_of_the_world/leaning_tower_of_pisa_facts/93/

Pisa map and guide Giusewppe Marrocchi Luglio 1990 p 9

Understanding Recounts

Circle a letter or write an answer for questions 1 to 7.

1. Including the ground floor how many storeys high is the Leaning Tower of Pisa?

   A   two   B   five   C   six   D   eight

2. The Tower is described as *freestanding* in the first paragraph.
   A freestanding tower is one that is

   A   constructed without proper safe guards
   B   built at no cost to the owner
   C   not attached to any other building
   D   a long distance from other buildings

3. How many arches around the second storey?

   Write the answer in the box. ☐

4. The Tower began to lean because

   A   the Tower took almost 200 years to build
   B   the soft ground had difficulty supporting the weight
   C   work on the Tower was stopped twice
   D   engineers didn't see there was a problem

5. Write the numbers 1 to 4 in the boxes to show the order in which building events occurred in the recount. The first one (1) has been done for you.

☐	construction stops at the second floor as the Tower begins to lean
☐	the Tower is given World Heritage listing
☐	the Tower is completed
1	construction begins on the Tower

6. This information would be most suitable for

   A   a history book   B   a builder's manual
   C   an atlas   D   a newsletter

7. In which year was it claimed that the Tower had finally stopped leaning further to one side?

   Write the date in the box. ☐

Lit Tip 27 – Improve your Literacy skills   Articles

When writing there are three articles to use: *the, an* and *a.*
The refers to a particular noun either singular or plural: the boy/ the boys.
The boy is a particular boy, not just any boy. *The* is called the *definite* article.
The may go before adjectives that describe nouns: the rude boy

Indefinite articles are *a* and *an.* They are used when we don't know or care which thing we are talking about. *A* boy was in the crowd. No particular boy, just a boy in the crowd.
An is used before singular nouns that begin with a vowel sound: *an eye*
Can you grasp the difference between these two sentences?
Angi saw a *thief* in the shop.   Angi saw the *thief* in the shop.

Understanding Year 3 Comprehension
A. Horsfield © Five Senses Education © W. Marlin

The Birthday Present

Tomorrow's Jasmine's birthday
And she'll be turning four.
She knows there's something hidden
Behind the garage door.

She saw it when she went to get
Her bike out of the shed.
It's wrapped in pretty paper
All green and blue and red.

It's in a box about as big
As Nanna's small TV.
She'd love to take a tiny peep
And see what she could see.

She knows it's not a puppy
'Cause she couldn't hear it bark.
She'd like to have a little dog
And take it to the park.

Perhaps it's full of books to read
She knows her ABC.
It might just be another doll.
Whatever could it be?

She tried to lift the corner up
To see if it would shake,
But it was far too heavy
And she thought that it might break.

So here she is in bed awake
Just staring at the door.
Tomorrow is her birthday
And she'll be turning ____(7)____.

Elaine Horsfield

Understanding Poetry

Circle a letter or write an answer for questions 1 to 7.

1. The present behind the garage door was most likely put there by

   A   Jasmine's Nanna   B   the owner of the puppy

   C   Jasmine's parents   D   a bike rider

2. Jasmine discovers her present when she was

   A   walking her puppy

   B   getting her bike from the shed

   C   playing with her dolls

   D   watching her Nanna's TV

3. How old is Jasmine on the day before her birthday?

   Write the answer in the box. ☐

4. Jasmine knew her present wasn't a puppy because

   A   she couldn't hear any barking

   B   the box rattled

   C   she peeped inside the box

   D   the box was too heavy

5. Jasmine lays in bed awake. (last verse)
   This is most likely because she is feeling

   A   lonely   B   worried   C   miserable   D   excited

6. Which word from the poem is a compound word? (Check **Lit Tip 17**.)

   A   garage   B   staring   C   birthday   D   present

7. A word has been deleted from the text.
   Which word would be best suited to the space (7)?

   A   more   B   four   C   older   D   five

Lit Tip 28 – Improve your Literacy skills   **Verb types**

Verbs are the most important part of a sentence.
You are often told that verbs are **action** words or doing words.
Some **action** verbs: jump, paint, chewing, writing and follow
Some verbs can be **thinking** words. There is no action involved.
Some **thinking** verbs: hope, think, understand, remember and decide
Some verbs are not doing or thinking. They tell about **being** something.
Some **being** verbs: is, are, was, am and were

Highlight the verbs in this verse from the poem. Can you name the verb types?

        She tried to lift the corner up
        To see if it would shake,
        But it was far too heavy
        And she thought that it might break.

Understanding Year 3 Comprehension
A. Horsfield © Five Senses Education © W. Marlin

Shoo Fly

Dad was reading his paper by our pool. A fly buzzed by. It circled dad's head. Dad rolled up his paper and took a swipe at it. 'Shoo fly, don't bother me!' he called. He missed the fly!

The fly buzzed around his head again. We have to get rid of that fly!' he growled. Dad took a big, BIG swipe. And missed again!

He knocked mum's hat off. Dad was shocked. Mum was shocked. She spilled her drink. She was not impressed.

The fly just laughed then buzzed by Mum. 'Shoo fly, don't bother me!' she called.

Mum tried to clap it in her hands. 'We have to get rid of that fly!' she growled. She missed the fly. Her book tumbled into the pool.

The fly just laughed and buzzed by me. It landed on my forehead. I waited and I thought, 'Shoo fly, don't bother me!

Suddenly I slapped my forehead. I missed the fly! 'Ouch!' I cried.

The fly just laughed and flew away. I followed it. I had to get rid of that fly. It buzzed by my dog Ditto. Ditto was resting in the shade of a lemon tree. It buzzed by his pointy ears.

Ditto growled. The fly landed on his tail. Ditto glared at it then snapped at it. Ditto missed the fly but bit his own tail! He yelped!

The fly just laughed and flew off into the garden. I have to get that darn fly!

Understanding Narratives

Circle a letter or write an answer for questions 1 to 7.

1. Who did the fly first annoy?

   A   Mum   B   Dad   C   Ditto   D   the child

2. Where was Ditto when he bit his own tail?

   A   he was near the father's seat
   B   he was by the pool
   C   he was under a lemon tree
   D   he was in the garden

3. How many times did Dad try to swipe the fly?
   Write your answer in the box.

4. Dad tried to get the fly by

   A   knocking it off Mum's hat
   B   swiping at it with a newspaper
   C   clapping his hands on it
   D   hitting it when it was on his forehead

5. What happened when Mum tried to hit the fly?

   A   she hit herself on the forehead
   B   she fell into the pool
   C   she chased after the fly
   D   she dropped her book into the pool

6. When Dad took a swipe at the fly he

   A   spilled his drink   B   laughed at the fly
   C   knocked Mum's hat off   D   pushed Ditto into the pool

7. Which word from the text has both a prefix and a suffix?
   (Check out **Lit Tip 24 and 26**.)

   A   snapped   B   impressed
   C   forehead   D   newspaper

Lit Tip 29 – Improve your Literacy skills   **Adjectives**

Adjectives are used to describe nouns: example, <u>dead</u> tree (noun).
Adjectives can tell the reader the quality (<u>large</u> tree), quantity (<u>many</u> trees) and number (<u>second</u> tree) of nouns.
You can have a series of adjectives: a few, small, young trees.
They are often separated by commas.
Adjectives do not have to come before the noun: the tree was <u>green</u>.

Underline the adjectives in this sentence.
It was a cool, spring morning on the tiny beach but the afternoon sun was hot.

Understanding Year 3 Comprehension
A. Horsfield © Five Senses Education © W. Marlin

What are Capers?

Capers are salty, pea-sized dark green cooking ingredients. They're commonplace especially in Mediterranean dishes such as pasta, but also in French dishes such as salade Nicoise. They give a salty, tart and vinegary bite to recipes. Do you know what capers actually are and where they come from?

Capers are pickled flower buds. Tiny capers are picked from a shrub-like bush (*Capparis spinosa*), long before the buds ever flower. They are not a fruit. They are dried in the sun and later brined (soaked in salty water) or packed in salt. Then they are packaged.

Some capers are allowed to mature to a fruit about the size of an olive. These are sold as caper berries and are brined to be eaten like pickles or olives.

Capers aren't new to the culinary scene - they've been around since ancient times. They're grown in parts of Asia, the Middle East, the Mediterranean, North Africa, Southern Europe, Turkey and California.

Harvesting capers is an arduous job because they can only be individually picked by hand. They're too small and delicate to be plucked by machine. That makes them expensive! The smallest size, called nonpareil, is the most desirable and most often used in recipes.

Next time you want to add some salty flavour to your dishes, try using capers. They're a perfect topping for fish, chicken or meat, and you can also use capers in a sauce, salad or on pizza. To use capers in recipes it's a good idea to rinse them first, to remove all the excess salt or brine.

Sources: http://www.huffingtonpost.com/2014/05/30/what-are-capers_n_1276491.html

Italian cookbook (title misplaced)

Pasta with capers

Understanding Explanations

Circle a letter to answer questions 1 to 7.

1. What are capers?

    A   a refreshing sauce for pizzas

    B   small bushes bearing peas

    C   a variety of Mediterranean olive

    D   pickled flower buds used in cooking

2. Capers are grown on

    A   a climbing vine   B   a small shrub

    C   a vegetable plant   D   a large fruit tree

3. What is brine?

    A   a salty water solution   B   a fruit the size of an olive

    C   a delicate caper flower   D   a tasty drink to have with pasta

4. To which dish is a chef most likely to add capers?

  A   B   C   D

5. Harvesting capers is an *arduous* job.

Which option provides the best meaning for *arduous* as used in the text?

    A   interesting and enjoyable   B   tiring and difficult

    C   rough and dangerous   D   confusing and tricky

6. Capers are picked by hand because

    A   cooks prefer hand picked capers

    B   the bushes can damage the machines

    C   pickers have to know what a caper looks like

    D   machine picking can spoil the caper

7. Before cooking with capers it is recommended that

    A   the small flowers are removed

    B   the seeds are separated from the berries

    C   salt is washed from the caper

    D   brine is added to the food

Lit Tip 30 – Improve your Literacy skills   There or their?

There and *their* sound the same but are spelled differently.

They are used in different ways. *There* is about place. *Their* is about ownership.

Examples: The Smiths had *their* car stolen.

             It was found over *there* by the creek.

Think of *here* and *there* as places. *Here* is part of *there*.

Complete these sentences with the right word.

1. The boys found _____ way home.   **2.** Don't go in _____ . It's unsafe!

Understanding Year 3 Comprehension
A. Horsfield © Five Senses Education © W. Marlin

Meg's Place

Meg lives in Gum Ridge. Her house is in Alan Drive.

GUM RIDGE TOWNSHIP

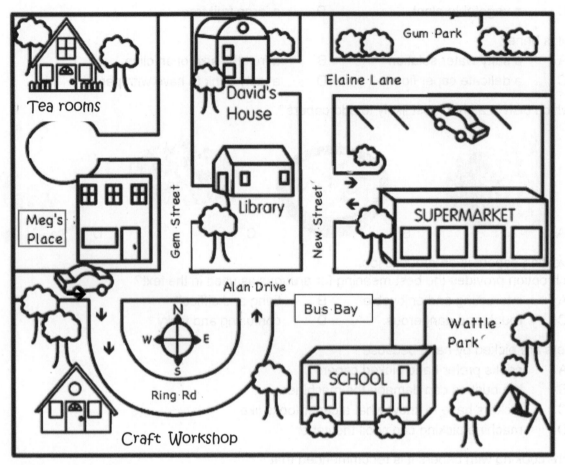

Adapted from a misplaced source

Understanding Maps

Circle a letter to answer questions 1 to 7.

1. Which street does the supermarket face?
   - A   Elaine Lane
   - B   Alan Drive
   - C   Gem Street
   - D   New Street

2. Which word would best describe the look of the *Tea rooms* building?
   - A   a cottage
   - B   an apartment
   - C   a cabin
   - D   a farmhouse

3. According to the map of Gum Ridge what is this place?
   - A   David' house
   - B   Craft workshop
   - C   Tea rooms
   - D   Library

4. Which street is most likely a one-way street?
   - A   Alan Drive
   - B   Ring Road
   - C   Elaine lane
   - D   Gem Street

5. Following the streets which is the best way for David to ride to school?
   - A   begin in Elaine Lane, turn right at New Street then turn right at Alan Street
   - B   go down Gem Street, cross Alan Drive and follow Ring Road to school
   - C   start in Elaine Lane, turn right into New Street then cross Alan Drive
   - D   start in Elaine Lane, turn left into New Street then cross Alan Drive

6. Who is likely to use the Bus Bay most often?
   - A   students attending the school
   - B   shoppers going to the supermarket
   - C   children going to the Wattle Park playground
   - D   visitors interested in craft activities

7. Meg wants to go to the craft workshop after school.
   Which direction is the craft workshop from the school?
   - A   north
   - B   south
   - C   east
   - D   west

Lit Tip 31 – Improve your Literacy skills   **Adverbs**

An **adverb** is often used to <u>add</u> meaning to <u>verbs</u>; ran (verb) quickly

Types of adverbs

Adverbs that tell **how**: sang softly, spoke clearly, badly injured

Many of these adverb types end with *ly*.

Adverbs of **time**: returned yesterday, left early, arrived soon

Adverbs of **place**: went below, there goes the alarm, here to help

Underline the adverbs in this sentence.

Soon the bus will move quickly and silently into the city.

Understanding Year 3 Comprehension
A. Horsfield © Five Senses Education © W. Marlin

The History of Transport

For humans, the first means of transport were walking and swimming. The taming of animals provided a new way to transport loads on sturdy creatures. Heavy loads could be hauled. Humans could ride animals at speed for long times. Inventions such as the wheeled cart and sled helped make animal transport more efficient through the use of "vehicles".

The first watercraft were canoes cut from tree trunks and rowed. Sailing vessels go back thousands of years. They were the only efficient way to move large loads over distances before the use of machines. Transport by water meant most cities were on rivers or by the sea, often where these two met.

Early forms of road transport were with horses, oxen or even humans carrying goods over dirt tracks that often followed animal trails. Paved roads were built by many early civilizations, including the Persians, Greeks and Romans. These empires built stone-paved roads so that armies could travel quickly. Deep roadbeds of crushed stone meant that the road surface did not turn to mud.

Until the age of machines, transport was slow and costly, and production and trading were as close to each other as practical.

Sources: Photo: http://en.wikipedia.org/wiki/File:Bullock_team.jpg

http://en.wikipedia.org/wiki/Transport

Understanding Recounts

Circle a letter to answer questions 1 to 7.

1. Which of these forms of human transport came first?
   - A   walking along tracks
   - B   rowing a canoe
   - C   sailing in a ship
   - D   horse riding

2. An early way to move heavy loads over great distances was by
   - A   bullock teams
   - B   machines with wheels
   - C   sailing ships
   - D   canoes cut from tree trunks

3. Which of these underlined words from the text is used as an adjective? (Check out **Lit Tip 29**)
   - A   <u>goes</u> back
   - B   <u>sturdy</u> creatures
   - C   travel <u>quickly</u>
   - D   wind for <u>propulsion</u>

4. The first paved roads were mainly built
   - A   to provide empires with food
   - B   to get goods to ships
   - C   for the use of bullock team drivers
   - D   to move troops quickly to battle areas

5. Heavy loads could be *hauled*.
   What is the meaning of hauled as used in paragraph 1?
   - A   prepared for removal
   - B   dragged or pulled with force
   - C   pushed from behind
   - D   carried to a destination

6. The text is a recount. This recount is intended to
   - A   give a description of types of "vehicle"
   - B   entertain the reader with details
   - C   retell events as they happened
   - D   advise the reader on how to move goods

7. Which would be the fastest form of transport for going a long distance?
   - A   riding a horse
   - B   rowing in a canoe
   - C   by foot
   - D   swimming

Lit Tip 32 – Improve your Literacy skills   **Here or hear?**

Hear and *here* sound the same but are spelled differently.
They are used in different ways. *Here* is about place. (Check out **Lit Tip 30**.) *Hear* is about sound.
Examples: We always come *here* for a swim.
            Did you *hear* the thunder last night?
Think about how you *hear*. You h<u>ear</u> with your <u>ear</u>.

Complete these sentences with the right word.

1. If you keep quiet I will _____ the music!

2. Come over _____ if you want to join in.

Look at these *Graphics.*

Graphics

Graphics refer to pictures and drawings. A **comic strip** is a series of drawings arranged in panels (sometimes called frames) to amuse or to form a narrative, often as a serial. Bubbles are used to show speech or thoughts. A cartoon is often a single picture intended to amuse. Captions and titles are sometimes included.

Text adapted from: http://en.wikipedia.org/wiki/Comic_strip
http://en.wikipedia.org/wiki/Cartoon, http://comics.azcentral.com/
http://needfulthings.hubpages.com/hub/calvin-hobbes 773709_f5209.JPG
Our thanks to Nancy Bevington for permission to reproduce graphic 1: nancybevington@bigpond.com
Information of how to contact actual copyright other holders would be appreciated by the writers.

Understanding Graphics

Circle a letter or write an answer for questions 1 to 7.

1. The comic strip and the cartoons are meant to
   - A provide the reader with information
   - B make the reader think about important things
   - C warn the reader of the dangers
   - D entertain the reader

2. How many panels in the comic strip Number **3**?

   Write your answer in the box. ☐

3. The clothes the man is wearing in Cartoon **1** suggest that he is
   - A a court jester
   - B going to a fancy dress party
   - C king of the land
   - D delivering a pizza

4. Look at the comic strip (Number **3**)
   What are the children doing?
   - A their homework
   - B a mathematics test
   - C writing a story
   - D waiting for their breakfast

5. What would be suitable words for the thought bubble in Cartoon **1**?
   - A When will my wife be home?
   - B Did someone knock?
   - C I must fix this door.
   - D What a lovely day!

6. In Cartoon **2** the teacher has this look on her face.
   This look suggests she is
   - A willing to do what the parents demand
   - B not sure she knows what the parents want
   - C shocked by being threatened
   - D annoyed with the parents' behaviour

7. A suitable caption for Cartoon **2** would be
   - A Satisfied parents
   - B Class teacher
   - C Parent - teacher night
   - D An understandable mistake!

Lit Tip 33 – Improve your Literacy skills   **Better words than *said***

Said is very easy to use when writing conversation.
There are many said words that can tell you more about how the character is feeling. Compare these sentences.

"Not again," chuckled Dad.   "Not again," groaned Dad.
"Not again," warned Dad.   "Not again," hissed Dad.
"Not again," joked Dad.   "Not again," yawned Dad.

It's a good idea to have your own list of *said* words.
Here are some to start you off: commanded, agreed, lied, whispered, urged

Understanding Year 3 Comprehension
A. Horsfield © Five Senses Education © W. Marlin

34 Read the poem *The Beach* by Elaine Horsfield.

This is Meg's poem about her visit to the beach.

The Beach

On sunny days the beach is fun.
The sand feels hot and makes me run.
The water's cold when I jump in,
But warms up when I start to swim.

The sun makes diamonds in the spray.
It's fun to watch the children play.
I see a ball drift out to sea.
A wave comes crashing over me.

I hear Dad call "It's time to eat!"
The sand goes squeak beneath my feet.
I watch the sea gulls squawk and fight.
They smell my bread and vegemite.

We hear the Mr Whippy man
And see him pull up in his van.
I love the smell of strawberry
And taste the cone Dad buys for me.

It dribbles down onto my chin.
The drips feel sticky on my skin
The sky looks like it's going to____(5)____.
I hope we'll soon come back again.

Elaine Horsfield

Understanding Poetry

Circle a letter or write an answer for questions 1 to 7.

1. What is the most likely time time Meg and her father were at the beach?
   - A early morning
   - B about lunchtime
   - C mid afternoon
   - D as the sun sets

2. Meg runs down the beach because (verse 1)
   - A the sand is hot under her feet
   - B she is in a hurry to buy an ice cream
   - C her father has called out to her
   - D she is chasing seagulls

3. What did Meg have on her sandwich?
   - A strawberry jam
   - B vegemite
   - C something sticky
   - D just butter

4. Which line from the poem suggests that the beach day was fine and warm?
   - A We hear the Mr Whippy man.
   - B I see a ball drift out to sea.
   - C The sand goes squeak beneath my feet.
   - D It's fun to watch the children play.

5. A word has been deleted from the poem.
   Which word would be best suited to the space (5)?
   - A Spain
   - B pour
   - C storm
   - D rain

6. Which word best describes Meg's day at the beach?
   - A enjoyable
   - B enchanting
   - C exhausting
   - D exciting

7. What was purchased from the Mr Whippy van?
   Write your answer in the line. _____.

Lit Tip 34 – Improve your Literacy skills

Between or among?

Between is most often used when two objects or people are involved.
Jill left the ball between the goal posts. (two goal posts)
Among involves more than two objects or people.
They found the ball among the weeds. (many weeds)

Underline the correct words to complete these sentences.
1. The coach was standing (among between) the players of the hockey team.
2. Let's keep this secret (among between) you and me.
3. Can you share the money (among between) Ron and Rosie?
4. The teachers were seen (among between) the high school students.

Understanding Year 3 Comprehension
A. Horsfield © Five Senses Education © W. Marlin

Gondwana Dreaming

Goopali gazed out to the sea and wondered if something other than more water existed beyond the horizon. Each season he noticed that birds arrived from faraway lands. Where were they from? Where did they go?

In summer Goopali speared fish in the shallow water or fished from his canoe. Yet, if his people could not drink the seawater why was there so much of it?

These questions troubled Goopali so much that one night a dream spirit visited him in his sleep. It led him to a vast open plain. Suddenly they sank below the plain where the evil spirits lived.

"Watch what is happening," said the dream spirit.

A huge battle waged between the evil spirits. It was so violent it caused the ground to tremble. Sections of the land began to break apart.

When they returned to the surface the ground before them opened up with a mighty roar. Rock thundered into the chasm.

"Is this the end of the world?" asked Goopali.

"No," explained the dream spirit. "This great land once split into two parts and drifted apart. One drifted to the other side of the sun. It was called Gondwana. In time parts of Gondwana broke off to form new lands. All that remains is this vast island where your people have lived for centuries.

"I knew it!" beamed Goopali. "There is land beyond the water!"

"True," said the spirit, "but much too far to reach in your canoe."

Adapted from: Even more tales my grandmother told me by Naiura Bartel Publications Australia 2010

Understanding Legends

Circle a letter to answer questions 1 to 7.

1. What made Goopali wonder if something existed beyond the horizon?
   - A   people had arrived from unexpected places in canoes
   - B   he could see nothing beyond the horizon
   - C   the evil spirits must have come from somewhere
   - D   strange birds arrived from far away places each season

2. Where was Goopali when the spirit visited?
   - A   on a plain
   - B   having a dream
   - C   under the earth
   - D   fishing in the shallow water

3. What happened to the land called Gondwana?
   - A   it was swallowed up in sea water
   - B   it drifted over the horizon
   - C   it sank below the plain
   - D   it split into two and drifted apart

4. Where did the evil spirits live?
   - A   on the other side of the sun
   - B   at the end of the world
   - C   below the plain
   - D   in a giant chasm

5. What did Goopali do after he saw the battle of evil spirits?
   - A   he rowed his canoe to the horizon
   - B   he visited the land called Gondwana
   - C   he returned to the surface of the ground
   - D   he drifted to the other side of the sun

6. Which word best describes Goopali?
   - A   disbelieving   B   curious   C   impatient   D   cautious

7. *Rock thundered into the chasm.*
   What is a *chasm*?
   - A   a deep crack in the ground
   - B   a place over the horizon
   - C   a volcanic crater
   - D   a high cliff

Lit Tip 35 – Improve your Literacy skills   Writing ordinal numbers

Ordinal numbers give the position in a series, such as first, second or third.
They have two main forms.

first - 1st	fourth - 4th	seventh - 7th	tenth - 10th
second- 2nd	fifth - 5th	eighth - 8th	eleventh - 11th
third - 3rd	sixth - 6th	ninth - 9th	twelfth - 12th

Monarchs have their ordinal numbers written as Roman numbers.
George I, Elizabeth II, Henry VIII. We say *the* before the ordinal: James <u>the</u> First.

Write the short ordinal for these numbers.

one _____, two _____, three _____, four _____

Understanding Year 3 Comprehension
A. Horsfield © Five Senses Education © W. Marlin

Parts of a Skateboard

Most beginning skaters buy a complete skateboard from a store. They are not really concerned with what the parts do.

Riders start to care when they have to repair their boards. They _really_ begin to care when they start becoming skilled skateboarders and realise that all those little parts actually help them to do what you want to do.

The Main Parts

A skateboard is made up of three main parts: a **deck**, **trucks** and **wheels**.

The deck the rider stands on is usually made of wood. The biggest differences are in size and shape. The skateboard deck has both an upturned nose and tail, and a curve shape through the middle. These features give a skateboarder greater control over how the board moves when doing tricks. Usually wider boards are used for ramp skating and narrower boards are used on the street.

Shape is mostly what the rider prefers, but size really matters. Riders want a deck that is the right length for the skateboarder's size and the right width for the skateboarder's feet and what they like to do. If they prefer doing tricks then a narrower deck will work best.

This diagram is a guide to what the parts are called.

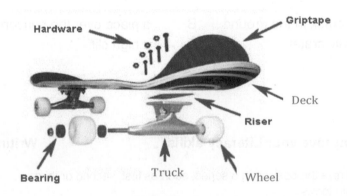

Sources: text: http://www.awesome-skateboard.com/SkateboardParts.html
Image: http://www.webanswers.com/post-images/D/D1/1108D665-CADD-13C0-E404165D5B948585.gif
http://entertainment.howstuffworks.com/skateboarding1.htm

Understanding Guides

Circle a letter or write an answer for questions 1 to 7.

1. How do most beginner skateboard riders get their first skateboard?
   - A   from a sale in the street
   - B   in parts to be assembled
   - C   complete from a store
   - D   at a skateboard ramp

2. The three main parts of a skateboard are the wheels, deck and the
   - A   trucks   B   griptape   C   bearings   D   riser

3. How many trucks does a skateboard have?

   Write your answer in the box. ☐

4. According to the text skateboard riders begin to take care of their boards when
   - A   a new model comes into the stores
   - B   they begin ramp skating
   - C   repairs are necessary
   - D   they ride in the streets

5. The importance of the upturned nose and tail is to
   - A   make the board more attractive
   - B   give the rider greater control of the board
   - C   prevent the rider's foot from slipping off
   - D   add strength to the wood

6. The writer has the word *really* in italics: They *really* start to care
   The word *really* is in italics because the writer
   - A   is unable to find a better word to show a difference
   - B   thinks it is something a skilled rider must know how to do
   - C   thinks beginner riders do not take proper care for their boards
   - D   wants to emphasise a difference between learners and skilled riders

7. According to the text what really matters about a skateboard deck is its
   - A   size   B   design   C   colour   D   nose

Lit Tip 36 – Improve your Literacy skills   **Writing the date**
(Check out **Lit Tip 35**)

When we **speak** of the date we usually say something like '22nd of January'.
We don't write it this way. In writing, we have several choices.
All numbers: 22/01/07, 22-01-07, 22/1/07, 22-1-07
With Letters and numbers the preferred method is: 22 January, 2007 OR
January 22, 2007.

The ordinal abbreviations are **not** included.

Write your birthday using numbers and word. _____

Understanding Year 3 Comprehension
A. Horsfield © Five Senses Education © W. Marlin

First Australian Eleven

From the early 1860s onwards, cricket matches between Aboriginal stockmen and European settlers had been played on the cattle stations in Western Victoria.

The athletic skills of the Aborigines were so evident that a strong Aboriginal eleven was formed.

This team travelled to England in 1868 for a series of matches against county teams. This was 10 years before the Australian Eleven travelled to England for the first official Test match on British soil. The first Australian cricket team to travel overseas was an Aboriginal team!

The team got mixed reactions from the English public. The Times newspaper described the tourists as unworthy to play on top English grounds. However matches were popular with the first match drawing 20,000 spectators. The entertainment included demonstrations of boomerang and spear throwing as well as cricket.

The 1868 Aboriginal cricket team wore uniforms of a red shirt and blue sash as well as distinctive caps so that spectators could tell them apart.

The Australians surprised their competitors with their skill, winning 14, losing 14 and drawing 19 of their 47 matches. Unaarrimin (also known as Johnny Mullagh) was the best player, scoring 1698 runs and taking 245 wickets.

Understanding Reports

Circle a letter or write an answer for questions 1 to 7.

1. As well as playing cricket in England the Aboriginal team
   - A   gave displays of Aboriginal hunting techniques
   - B   visited *The Times* newspaper
   - C   took part in the first official test in Britain
   - D   went to a match on a top cricket ground

2. The word *Eleven* in the title ***First Australian Eleven*** is
   - A   the number of English matches the Australians played
   - B   another name for any cricket team
   - C   the number of wins the visitors had
   - D   it was the time in weeks that the tour lasted

3. What was unusual about the 1868 Aboriginal cricket tour?
   - A   it was played on top British cricket grounds
   - B   the men had never played cricket before the tour
   - C   the players were a mixture of European settlers
   - D   it was the first Australian team to play overseas

4. The aboriginal team played English *county* teams.
   A *county* team is one that
   - A   is the best in the country
   - B   is located in a capital city
   - C   comes from a rural area
   - D   plays official matches

5. How many wickets did Unaarrimin take during the tour?

   Write your answer in the box. ☐

6. Which option best describes how the tour could be considered?
   - A   it was treated as an absurd event
   - B   it failed to create much interest
   - C   it was surprisingly popular
   - D   it upset many cricketers

7. How many matches did the 1868 Aboriginal team win?
   - A   11   B   14   C   19   D   27

Lit Tip 37 – Improve your Literacy skills   **Correct usage – alot and brung**

The word *alot* does not exist. It is often mistakenly written instead of *a lot*.

Incorrect: I know *alot* of names. ✖   **Correct:** I know *a lot* of names. ✔

The word *brang* does not exist. It is often mistakenly said instead of *brought*.

The past tense of *bring* is *brought* **not** *brung* or *brang*.

Incorrect: I *brung* my book home. ✖   **Correct:** I *brought* my book home. ✔

Write the correct words in the spaces.

1. I sing _____ in the shower.   2. Tom _____ the cat inside.

Understanding Year 3 Comprehension
A. Horsfield © Five Senses Education © W. Marlin

Read the procedure *How to Use a String Knife.*

How to Use a String Knife

Can a string really cut ice? Yes, you can "cut" through a piece of ice using only a piece of strong string. You could safely conduct this experiment in the family kitchen.

> This experiment uses gravity and time – and practice!

Science Concept

Ice is frozen water. By itself, ice tends to stay frozen, unless it is heated. But other things can cause ice to melt – pressure is one.

This experiment uses pressure of a piece of string to melt part of a block of ice, and then to move through that melted portion, and allow the ice to refreeze behind it. The string moves its way through the ice, as if it were cutting it.

Materials

- a largish ice block
- 1 sturdy plastic glass
- 1 piece of strong thin string, about 30 cm long
- 2 similar objects for weights

Procedure

1. Carefully balance an ice block on top of the plastic glass.
2. Tie a weight to each end of the string and carefully hang it across the top of the ice block.
3. Over time, the string should pass through the ice until it finally passes completely through.

This weird happening is called *regelation*. It is what happens when ice melts under pressure and freezes again when the pressure is removed.

Sources: http://en.wikipedia.org/wiki/Regelation
http://www.netplaces.com/kids-magical-science-experiments/running-hot-and-cold/string-knifequestion-can-a-string-cut-ice.htm

Understanding Procedures

Circle a letter or write an answer for questions 1 to 7.

1. What happens to the ice block as the string "cuts" its way through?
   - A   it holds the string in one place
   - B   it breaks into parts
   - C   it refreezes along the "cut" line
   - D   it begins to melt rapidly

2. Most people would find the results of this experiment
   - A   amusing
   - B   foolish
   - C   alarming
   - D   unexpected

3. When you cut through a piece of ice using the method described you get two pieces of ice.

   Is this TRUE or FALSE?   Tick a box.   TRUE ☐   FALSE ☐

4. In this experiment what has be done after the string with weights has been placed over the ice block?
   - A   wait patiently
   - B   hold the ice block steady
   - C   stop the glass from falling over
   - D   remove any scraps of ice

5. This experiment would be useful in showing
   - A   ice blocks can balance on a glass
   - B   ice can melt under pressure
   - C   string can cut better than a knife
   - D   heat is needed to melt ice

6. According to the text a suitable place to do this experiment would be in
   - A   a workshop
   - B   a science laboratory
   - C   an outdoor area
   - D   a home kitchen

7. How many items are required to complete the experiment?
   - A   three   B   four   C   five   D   six

Lit Tip 38 – Improve your Literacy skills   **Direct speech** (Check out **Lit Tip 33**)

Direct speech is the actual words spoken.
To write direct speech correctly you need a capital letter, inverted commas (2) (quotation marks), some punctuation and a full stop.

open inverted commas   closed inverted commas   full stop

capital letter —— "What is your name?" asked the teacher.

punctuation (?)

This is just one of many ways to write direct speech.
The punctuation separating the two parts could also be a comma or an exclamation mark. They always go inside the inverted commas.

Add all the punctuation to this sentence: I am here for the bag said Eve

Understanding Year 3 Comprehension
A. Horsfield © Five Senses Education © W. Marlin

Graffiti is Great

Do you like graffiti? I think it's great! It is the art of modern times. It is certainly better than some of those old fashioned, drab portraits and those religious pictures done centuries ago.

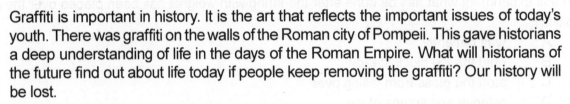

Why do I like it? Firstly I like the bright colours and the swirling designs. People who call it rubbish just haven't looked at it closely. The designs and patterns are intricate and bold. Sometimes the work of graffiti artists is amusing.

Graffiti is important in history. It is the art that reflects the important issues of today's youth. There was graffiti on the walls of the Roman city of Pompeii. This gave historians a deep understanding of life in the days of the Roman Empire. What will historians of the future find out about life today if people keep removing the graffiti? Our history will be lost.

What do you think looks the best? Boring old grey concrete walls? Boring, dirty old brick housing units? Public buildings where the paintwork is old and flaking? No, thank you! I like fresh, brightly painted____(6)____.

Graffiti artists are doing us a service. They are helping to make the place more attractive as well as protecting surfaces with a fresh coat of paint. Graffiti is not vandalism.

Finally the messages a lot of graffiti artist leave behind are ones of love, hope and peace. They want society to be a better place. It's about time councils stopped removing graffiti from our towns and cities and treating it as the art of real people!

Understanding Opinions

1. Which option best describes the writer's attitude to graffiti?

   A   graffiti is a form of vandalism
   B   graffiti has historical value
   C   graffiti provides councils with work
   D   graffiti should be removed from walls

2. What is one thing the writer dislikes?

   A   the messages included in graffiti   B   historians removing graffiti
   C   learning about Ancient Rome   D   drab religious portraits

3. The writer states that graffiti is not *vandalism*.
   What is *vandalism*?

   A   any criticism of the work of graffiti artists
   B   the protection of walls with fresh paint
   C   any deliberate damaging of property
   D   the painting of designs with bright swirls

4. Why was the Roman city of Pompeii important to the writer?

   A   it was a great Roman city
   B   it showed that graffiti has value
   C   it explained the origins of graffiti
   D   it provided an example of youth interests

5. The writer describes graffiti as *intricate*. Graffiti that is *intricate* is

   A   detailed   B   valuable   C   common   D   drab

6. A word has been deleted from the text.
   Which word would be best suited to the space (6)?

   A   faces   B   surfaces   C   rubbish   D   portraits

7. Which of these would the writer of the text most likely prefer?

   A   B   C   D

Lit Tip 39 - Improve your Literacy skills   **Indirect speech** (Check out **Lit Tip** **38.**)

Indirect speech (or reported speech) is used to show what someone has said without using the exact words.
Compare: Kate said, "I walked home." / Kate said that she had walked home.
Bob asked, "Is my father is ill?" / Bob asked if his father was ill.
Indirect speech does not need quotation marks.

Rewrite these sentences using indirect speech.

1. Sue said, "I was hot at school," _____

2. Bev asked, "Do you know the time?" _____

Miserable Merve

Mervin was at home, but he was not alone. He felt as if he was alone because he was bored and miserable. Being bored made him feel tired just sitting at the table.

He sat, spinning his knife around on the table top, and not eating his food. It was spaghetti and meatballs. The spaghetti was cold and gluggy like long, cold, dirty red worms. He wasn't going to eat half-dead worms of spaghetti! It made his tummy go tight just thinking about it.

He stopped spinning his knife and said in his most polite voice, "Mum, do you think I could go and see Uncle Jack next week seeing I'm not allowed to go tomorrow?"

Mervin's mother did not reply immediately. She was sucking up the long last bit of her spaghetti into her mouth. Mervin pulled a face as if he was going to be sick.

When the red worm finally disappeared into her mouth she swallowed it then looked at Mervin for a few moments as if she was thinking about something important. When she finally spoke her voice was quiet and definite.

"Mervin, we have been through this a million times. You know I believe it's in your best interests that you and Uncle Jack don't get together for quite a while. His crackpot schemes will end up with someone in the police lock-up - or the mad house."

Mervin's shoulders slumped even further and he gave the knife another spin.

"Just finish your spaghetti like a good little boy," his mother said sweetly.

"Not a good *little* boy," mumbled Mervin.

Understanding Narratives

Circle a letter to answer questions 1 to 7.

1. Mervin spun his knife around on the table because he was feeling

   A   sick   B   impatient   C   bored   D   naughty

2. What is the most likely reason that Mervin's spaghetti was cold and gluggy?

   A   he was late getting to the dinner table
   B   he didn't eat it when his mother first served it
   C   he preferred his spaghetti that way
   D   he was waiting for Uncle Jack to come

3. What was Mervin's mother's opinion of Uncle Jack?

   A   he was reliable   B   he was great fun
   C   he was well organised   D   he was eccentric

4. Mervin's mother describes Uncle Jack's schemes as *crackpot schemes*?
   A *crackpot scheme* is one that is

   A   liable to end in failure   B   well planned
   C   extremely dangerous   D   fun to take on

5. When Mervin was told he could not visit Uncle Jack his *shoulders slumped.*
   When Mervin's *shoulders slumped* this means he was feeling

   A   grateful   B   disappointed   C   sleepy   D   foolish

6. Which option is an example of a simile as used in the text?

   A   sucking up the long last bit of her spaghetti
   B   we have been through this a million times
   C   cold and gluggy like long, cold, dirty red worms
   D   he gave the knife another spin

7. It is most likely Mervin feels miserable because he

   A   is not allowed to visit Uncle Jack
   B   has to watch his mother eat spaghetti
   C   doesn't like meatballs with spaghetti
   D   was called a little boy by his mother

Lit Tip 40 - Improve your Literacy skills   **Alliteration**

Alliteration is the use of the same letter or sound at the beginning of words that are close
together in the text, especially poetry but also in other text: green grass, dainty daisies,
Miserable Merve

Alliteration can be used to add interest to your story writing.

Look at the letters that are used for alliteration in these examples.

1. slip and slide   2. windy wasteland   3. big, bad Ben

Add an adjective to these nouns to make examples of alliteration.

1. _____ pig, **2.** _____ road, **3.** _____ duck, **4.** _____ coffee

Alliteration can be used effectively for words that resemble sounds - We heard the horses clip, clop
down the street.

Understanding Year 3 Comprehension
A. Horsfield © Five Senses Education © W. Marlin

SOLUTIONS

ANSWERS - Reading Comprehension Tests   84, 85

ANSWERS - Literacy Tip Exercises   86, 87

Understanding Year 3 Comprehension
A. Horsfield © Five Senses Education © W. Marlin

Answers
Year 3 Comprehension Questions

No.	Title	Answers

1. Daintree River Ferry: 1. A   2. Mossman   3. B   4. D   5. C   6. C   7. B

2. What is a Bunyip?   1. A   2. B   3. B   4. D   5. C   6. A   7. D

3. Shopping with Dad: 1. A   2. B   3. C   4. D   5. B   6. while (also smile)   7. C

4. The Mice's Meeting: 1. C   2. B   3. A   4. D   5. FALSE   6. A   7. B

5. Wash Your Hands!:   1. A   2. NO   3. C   4. A   5. (2, 3, 1, 4)   6. D   7. B

6. Olivia's Birthday Invitation: 1. C   2. A   3. Judy   4. C   5. D   6. B   7. D

7. The Cassowary: 1. A   2. A   3. cassowary   4. C   5. B   6. D   7. B

8. Leap Year Day: 1. D   2. B   3. FALSE   4. A   5. C   6. A   7. B

9. Dad's Lesson: 1. B   2. A   3. D   4. C   5. B   6. D   7. C

10. Rock Ringtail Possum: 1. B   2. C   3. D   4. A   5. D   6. C   7. A

11. The Bone: 1. C   2. B   3. C   4. B   5. (3, 2, 4, 1)   6. D   7. A

12. Taps for Tinies: 1. B   2. A   3. C   4. D   5. A   6. D   7. B

13. Rhys: 1. A   2. C   3. D   4. holiday   5. A   6. C   7. B

14. Searching for Monsters: 1. D   2. A   3. B   4. C   5. A   6. D   7. before

15. Mimic Octopus: 1. C   2. A   3. B   4. C   5. A   6. B   7. more than 15

16. Mangroves: 1. D   2. C   3. B   4. A   5. D   6. C   7. A

17. Kids in Supermarkets: 1. A   2. B   3. D   4. A   5. B   6. C   7. C

18. Honeycomb Slice Recipe: 1. C   2. B   3. D   4. A   5. (3, 2, 4, 1)   6. D   7. C

19. Old Mike: 1. A   2. C   3. B   4. A   5. D   6. D   7. B

20. Heteronyms: 1. A   2. B   3. B   4. D   5. C   6. D   7. A

Continued on the next page...

21. Marsupial Lion: 1. A 2. B 3. C 4. A 5. B 6. D 7. C

22. Crocodile: 1. D 2. B 3. (smile, while or reptile) 4. D 5. C 6. B 7. A

23. Paddington: 1. B 2. D 3. Peru 4. A 5. C 6. B 7. B

24. Ginga: 1. D 2. C 3. A 4. D 5. B 6. D 7. B

25. Growing Seeds: 1. D 2. C 3. D 4. B 5. C 6. B 7. A

26. Types of Whistles: 1. B 2. A 3. C 4. D 5. A 6. C 7. D

27. Leaning Tower of Pisa: 1. D 2. C 3. (30) 4. B 5. (2, 4, 3, 1) 6. A 7. 2008

28. The Birthday Present: 1. C 2. B 3. (3) 4. A 5. D 6. C 7. B

29. Shoo Fly: 1. B 2. C 3. (2) 4. B 5. D 6. C 7. B

30. What are Capers? 1. D 2. B 3. A 4. C 5. B 6. D 7. C

31. Meg's Place: 1. B 2. A 3. D 4. B 5. C 6. A 7. D

32. The History of Transport: 1. A 2. C 3. B 4. D 5. B 6. C 7. A

33. Graphics: 1. D 2. (4) 3. C 4. B 5. B 6. A 7. D

34. The Beach: 1. B 2. A 3. B 4. C 5. D 6. A 7. (strawberry) ice cream

35. Gondwana Dreaming: 1. D 2. B 3. D 4. C 5. C 6. B 7. A

36. Parts of a Skateboard: 1. C 2. A 3. (2) 4. C 5. B 6. D 7. A

37. First Australian Eleven: 1. A 2. B 3. D 4. C 5. (245) 6. C 7. B

38. How to Use a String Knife: 1. C 2. D 3. FALSE 4. A 5. B 6. D 7. C

39. Graffiti: 1. B 2. D 3. C 4. B 5. A 6. B 7. D

40. Miserable Merve: 1. C 2. B 3. D 4. A 5. B 6. C 7. A

Understanding Year 3 Comprehension
A. Horsfield © Five Senses Education © W. Marlin

Year 3 Answers

Lit Tips Exercises

No. Text title	Topic	Answers
1. Daintree River Ferry	Capitalisation	We Sir Peter Green Perth Sunday He Big Mac
2. What is a Bunyip?	Alphabetical order 1	1. H, N, 2. S, X, 3. seal
3. Shopping with Dad	Rhyme	1. low 2. said 3. pure 4. home
4. The Mice's Meeting	Alphabetical order 2	1. 5, 4, 1, 2, 3 2. 4, 2, 1, 5, 3
5. Wash Your Hands!	Full stops	Between: *day. Lee's, wet. Mine, dry. They* and after *cleaning.*
6. Olivia's Invitation	Question marks	1. (?) 2. (.)
7. The Cassowary	Exclamation marks	No response for the exercise is required.
8. Leap Year Day	Common nouns	shirt, cap, sunlight, line, pegs
9. Dad's Lesson	Proper nouns	Easter, Ken, Jetstar, Bribie Island Queensland, Examples: Perth, Africa
10. Rock Ringtail Possum	Synonyms	1. lovely (suggestion) 2. big-large, sad-glum, noisy-rowdy, rich-wealthy, clever-smart, answer-reply
11. The Bone	Antonyms	1. first 2. fast-slow, dark-light, noisy-quiet, dead-alive, true-false, answer-ask 3. <u>un</u>fair
12. Taps for Tinies	Ordinals	6th, 9th, 23rd, 11th
13. Rhys	Writer or narrator?	No written responses required.
14. Searching for Monsters	Contractions	it is, you are, is not, let us, I would, *woul*
15. Mimic Octopus	Singular or plural	foxes, ghosts, bites, quizzes six, ash, cake, waltz, octopuses, tentacles
16. What are Mangroves?	Odd plurals	teeth, men, mice
17. Kids in Supermarkets	Compound words	something, supermarkets, hopeless, pretend, advice
18. Honeycomb Slice Recipe	Better words than got	1. *fetched* or *retrieved* 2. *grabbed* or *took* Suggestions: *climbed, fell, slipped* or *jumped*
19. Old Mike	Ownership by one	dog's bark, Sue's smile, lady's bag, man's hat, Dr Low's fee, fox's ears
20. Heteronyms	Heteronyms	Examples only: <u>Lead</u> is a grey metal. Dad can <u>lead</u> the horse.

Continued on the next page...

No. Text title	Topic	Answers
21. Marsupial Lion	Possession by many	babies, witches, boxes, boys' party, babies' mother, parents' home,
22. Crocodile	Use of commas	1. (3 commas) Dogs, cats, pigs, 2. (2 commas) cups, glasses, 3. No commas required.
23. Paddington	Affixes	1. ly, dis, pre, ing 2. recover<u>ed,</u> <u>tri</u>cycle<u>s,</u> <u>un</u>help<u>ful,</u> hope<u>less</u>/<u>ness</u>
24. Ginga	Prefixes	uncover, recover, discover
25. Growing Seeds	Short form for month names	September
26. Whistles	Suffixes	Examples: careless, careful, cares
27. Leaning Tower of Pisa	The articles	No written response
28. Birthday Present	Verb types	tried, lift, see, (would) shake, was, thought, break
29. Shoo Fly	Adjectives	cool, spring, tiny, afternoon, hot
30. What are Capers?	*There* or *their*?	1. their 2. there
31. Meg's Place	Adverbs	soon, quickly, silently
32. History of Transport	*Here* or *hear*?	1. hear 2. here
33. Graphics	Better words than said	No written responses required
34. The Beach	*Between* or *among*?	1. among 2. between 3. between 4. among
35. Gondwana Dreaming	Ordinal numbers	first, second, third, fourth
36. Parts of a Skateboard	Writing the date	Responses will vary
37. First Australian Eleven	Correct usage: *alot, brang*	1. a lot 2. brought
38. How to Use a String Knife	Direct speech	"I am here for the bag," said Eve.
39. Graffiti	Indirect speech	1. Sue said (that) she was hot at school. 2. Bev asked if I knew the time.
40. Miserable Merve	Alliteration	Suggestions: pink pig, rocky road, dead duck, cold coffee

Notes